COLONIAL AND POSTCOLONIAL
EAST AND SOUTHEAST
ASIA

EDITED BY
JULIA CHANDLER

Britannica®
Educational Publishing
IN ASSOCIATION WITH
ROSEN
EDUCATIONAL SERVICES

Published in 2017 by Britannica Educational Publishing (a trademark of Encyclopædia Britannica, Inc.) in association with The Rosen Publishing Group, Inc.
29 East 21st Street, New York, NY 10010

Distributed exclusively by Rosen Publishing.
To see additional Britannica Educational Publishing titles, go to rosenpublishing.com.

First Edition

Britannica Educational Publishing
J.E. Luebering: Executive Director, Core Editorial
Anthony L. Green: Editor, Compton's by Britannica

Rosen Publishing
Meredith Day: Editor
Nelson Sá: Art Director
Michael Moy: Designer
Cindy Reiman: Photography Manager
Bruce Donnola: Photo Researcher

Library of Congress Cataloging-in-Publication Data

Names: Chandler, Julia, 1988- editor.
Title: Colonial and Postcolonial East and Southeast Asia / edited by Julia Chandler.
Description: First edition. | New York : Britannica Educational Publishing in association with Rosen Educational Services, 2017. | Series: The colonial and postcolonial experience | Audience: Grades 7 to 12. | Includes bibliographical references and index.
Identifiers: LCCN 2016021834 | ISBN 9781508104384 (library bound : alkaline paper)
Subjects: LCSH: East Asia—Colonization—History—Juvenile literature. | Southeast Asia—Colonization—History—Juvenile literature. | Postcolonialism—East Asia—History—Juvenile literature. | Postcolonialism—Southeast Asia—History—Juvenile literature. | Europe—Colonies—Asia—History—Juvenile literature.
Classification: LCC DS511 .C787 2017 | DDC 950/.3--dc23
LC record available at https://lccn.loc.gov/2016021834

Manufactured in Malaysia

CONTENTS

The regions of East and Southeast Asia cover a wide swath of territory and different cultures. East Asia is usually considered to encompass China, Japan, Korea, and Mongolia, while Southeast Asia covers the region east of the Indian subcontinent and south of China. Mainland Southeast Asia is divided into the modern-day countries of Cambodia, Laos, Myanmar (Burma), Thailand, Vietnam, and the small city-state of Singapore at the southern tip of the Malay Peninsula; Cambodia, Laos, and Vietnam, which occupy the eastern portion of the mainland, often are collectively called the Indochinese Peninsula. Malaysia is both mainland and insular, with a western portion on the Malay Peninsula and an eastern part on the island of Borneo. Except for the small sultanate of Brunei (also on Borneo), the remainder of insular Southeast Asia consists of the archipelagic nations of Indonesia and the Philippines.

Colonialism across much of these regions began at the end of the 19th century as European nations and Japan spread their influence and control throughout the continent of Asia. Siam, as Thailand was officially called until 1939, was never brought under European colonial domination, but the rest of East Asia and Southeast Asia experienced some degree of colonialism from European nations, the United

The colonial experience across East and Southeast Asia varied; some areas were under colonial rule for centuries, while others were relatively unaffected.

States, or Japan. The evolution of the penetration of Asia was naturally influenced by a multiplicity of factors—economic and political conditions in the expanding nations, the strategy of the military officials of the latter nations, the problems facing colonial rulers in each locality, pressures arising from white settlers and businessmen in the colonies, as well as the constraints imposed by the always limited economic and military resources of the imperialist powers. All these elements were present to a greater or lesser extent at each stage of the forward push of the colonial frontiers by the Dutch in Indonesia, the French in Indochina (Vietnam, Laos, Cambodia), and the British in Malaya, Burma, and Borneo.

Yet, despite the variety of influences at work, three general types of penetration stand out. One of these is expansion designed to overcome resistance to foreign rule. Resistance, which assumed many forms ranging from outright rebellion to sabotage of colonial political and economic domination, was often strongest in the border areas farthest removed from the centres of colonial power. The consequent extension of military control to the border regions tended to arouse the fears and opposition of neighbouring states or tribal societies and thus led to the further extension of control. Hence, attempts to achieve military security prompted the addition of border areas and neighbouring nations to the original colony.

A second type of expansion was a response to the economic opportunities offered by exploitation of the colonial interiors. Traditional trade and the free play of market forces in Asia did not produce huge supplies of raw materials and food or the enlarged export markets sought by the industrializing colonial powers. For this, entrepreneurs and capital from abroad were needed, mines and plantations had to be organized, labour supplies mobilized, and money economies created. All these alien intrusions functioned best under the firm security of an accommodating alien law and order.

The third type of expansion was the result of rivalry among colonial powers. When possible, new territory was acquired or old possessions extended in order either to preclude occupation by rivals or to serve as buffers for military security against the expansions of nearby colonial powers. Where the crosscurrents of these rivalries prevented any one power from obtaining exclusive control, various substitute arrangements were arrived at: parts of a country were chipped off and occupied by one or more of the powers; spheres of influence were partitioned; unequal commercial treaties were imposed—while the countries subjected to such treatment remained nominally independent.

The penetration of China is the outstanding example of this type of expansion. In the early 19th century the middle part of eastern Asia (Japan, Korea, and China), containing about half the Asian population, was still little affected by Western penetration. By the end of the century, Korea was on the way to becoming annexed by Japan, which had itself become a leading imperialist power. China remained independent politically, though it was already extensively dominated by outside powers. Undoubtedly, the intense rivalry of the foreign powers helped save China from being taken over outright (as India had been). China was pressed on all sides by competing powers anxious for its trade and territory: Russia from the north, Great Britain (via India and Burma) from the south and west, France (via Indochina) from the south, and Japan and the United States (in part, via the Philippines) from the east.

The first phase of the forceful penetration of China by western Europe came in the two Opium Wars. Great Britain had been buying increasing quantities of tea from China, but it had few products that China was interested in buying by way of exchange. An increasing Chinese addiction to opium fed a boom in imports of the drug and led to an unfavourable trade balance paid for by a steady loss of China's silver reserves. In light of the economic effect of the opium trade plus the physical and mental deterioration of opium users, Chinese authorities banned the opium trade.

In June 1840 the British fleet arrived at the mouth of the Canton River to begin the Opium War. The Chinese capitulated in 1842 after the fleet reached the Yangtze, Shanghai fell, and Nanking was under British guns. The resulting Treaty of Nanking—the first in a series of commercial treaties China was forced to sign over the years—provided for: (1) cession of Hong Kong to the British crown; (2) the opening of five treaty ports, where the British would have residence and trade rights; (3) the right of British nationals in China who were accused of criminal acts to be tried in British courts; and (4) the limitation of duties on imports and exports to a modest rate. Other countries soon took advantage of this forcible opening of China; in a few years similar treaties were signed by China with the United States, France, and Russia.

The Western powers took advantage of China's increasing difficulties by pressing for even more favourable trade treaties, culminating in a second war against China (1856–60), this time by France and England. China's defeat in the second war with the West produced a series of treaties, signed at Tientsin with Britain, France, Russia, and the United States, which brought the Western world deeper into China's affairs. The Tientsin treaties provided, among other things, for the right of foreign nationals to travel in the interior, the right of foreign ships to trade and patrol on the Yangtze River, the opening up of more treaty ports, and additional exclusive legal jurisdiction by foreign powers over their nationals residing in China.

Treaties of this general nature were extended over the years to grant further privileges to foreigners. Furthermore, more and more Western nations—including Germany, Italy, Denmark, The Netherlands, Spain, Belgium, and Austria-Hungary—took advantage of the new opportunities by signing such treaties. By the beginning of the 20th century, some 90 Chinese ports had been opened to foreign control. In most of the treaty ports, China leased substantial areas of land at low rates to foreign governments. The consulates in these concessions exercised legal jurisdiction over their nationals, who thereby escaped China's laws and tax collections. The foreign settlements had their own police forces and tax systems and ran their own affairs independently of nominally sovereign China.

In any event, preliminary attempts to Westernize Chinese society from within did not deter further foreign penetration; nor did the subsequent revolution (1911) succeed in freeing China from Western domination. Toward the end of the 19th century, under the impact of the new imperialism, the spread of foreign penetration accelerated. Germany entered a vigorous bid for its sphere of influence; Japan and Russia pushed forward their territorial claims; and U.S. commercial and financial penetration of the Pacific, with naval vessels patrolling Chinese rivers, was growing rapidly.

But at the same time this mounting foreign interest also inhibited the outright partition of China. Any step by one of the powers toward outright partition or sizable enlargement of its sphere of influence met with strong opposition from other powers. This led eventually to the Open Door policy, advocated by the United States, which limited or restricted exclusive privileges of any one power vis-à-vis the others. It became generally accepted after the antiforeign Boxer Rebellion (1900) in China. With the foreign armies that had been brought in to suppress the rebellion now stationed in North China, the danger to the continued existence of the Chinese government and the danger of war among the imperialist powers for their share of the country seemed greater than ever. Agreement on the Open Door policy helped to retain both a compliant native government and equal opportunity for commerce, finance, and investment by the more advanced nations.

Japan was the only East Asian country to escape colonization from the West. European nations and the United States tried to "open the door," and to some extent they succeeded; but Japan was able to shake off the kind of subjugation, informal or formal, to which the rest of Asia succumbed. Even more important, it moved onto the same road of industrialization as did Europe and the United States. And instead of being colonized it became one of the colonial powers.

Japan had traditionally sought to avoid foreign intrusion. For many years, only the Dutch and the Chinese were allowed trading depots, each having access to only one port. No other foreigners were permitted to land in Japan, though Russia, France, and England tried, but with little success. The first significant crack in Japan's trade and travel barriers was forced by the United States in an effort to guarantee and strengthen its shipping interests in the Far East. Japan's guns and ships were no match for those of Commodore Perry in his two U.S. naval expeditions to Japan (1853, 1854).

The Japanese, well aware of the implications of foreign penetration through observing what was happening to China, tried to limit Western trade to two ports. In 1858, however, Japan agreed to a full commercial treaty with the United States, followed by similar treaties with the Low Countries, Russia, France, and Britain. The treaty pattern was familiar: more ports were opened; resident foreigners were granted extraterritorial rights, as in China; and import and export duties were predetermined, thus removing control that Japan might otherwise exercise over its foreign trade.

Many attempts have been made to explain why a weak Japan was not taken over as a colony or, at least, did not follow in China's footsteps. Despite the absence of a commonly accepted theory, two factors were undoubtedly crucial. On the one hand, the Western nations did not pursue their attempts to control Japan as aggressively as they did elsewhere. When greater interest developed in a possible breakthrough in Japan in the 1850s and 1860s, the leading powers were occupied with other pressing affairs, such as the 1857 Indian mutiny, the Taiping Rebellion, the Crimean War, French intervention in Mexico, and the U.S. Civil War. International jealousy may also have played a role in deterring any one power from trying to gain exclusive control over the country.

On the other hand, in Japan itself, the overthrow of the Tokugawa government and the restoration of the rule of the emperor Meiji brought new interest groups to the centre of political power and instigated a radical redirection of Japan's economic development. The nub of the changeover was the destruction of the traditional feudal social system and the building of a political, social, and economic framework conducive to capitalist industrialization. The ensuing industrialized economy provided the means for Japan to hold its own in modern warfare and to withstand foreign economic competition.

Soon Japan not only followed the Western path of internal industrialization, but it also began an outward aggression resembling that of the European nations. First came the acquisition and colonization of neighbouring islands: the Ryukyu Islands (including Okinawa), the Kuril Islands, Bonin Islands, and Hokkaido. Next in Japan's expansion program was Korea, but the opposition of other powers postponed the transformation of Korea into a Japanese colony. The pursuit of influence in Korea involved Japan in war with China (1894–95), at the end of which China recognized Japan's interest in Korea and ceded to Japan Taiwan, the Pescadores, and southern Manchuria.

At this point rival powers interceded to force Japan to forgo taking over the southern Manchuria peninsula. While France, Britain, and Germany were involved in seeking to frustrate Japan's imperial ambitions, the most direct clash was with Russia over Korea and Manchuria. Japan's defeat of Russia in the war of 1904–05 procured for Japan the lease of the Liaodong Peninsula, the southern part of the island of Sakhalin, and recognition of its "paramount interest" in Korea. Still, pressure by Britain and the United States kept Japan from fulfillment of its plan to possess Manchuria outright. By the early 20th century, however, Japan had, by means of economic and political penetration, attained a privileged position in that part of China, as well as colonies in Korea and Taiwan and neighbouring islands.

Japan conquered its Greater East Asia Co-prosperity Sphere and arrived at the gates of India, displacing British, Dutch, and French colonial rulers as well as the Americans in Guam and the Philippines. The Japanese had to allow some margin of freedom to their satellite regimes in Burma and Indonesia in both of which preexisting local parties proved capable of creating sovereign states after the war. On Aug. 17, 1945, Sukarno declared Indonesia independent. Indonesia had had a long history of Muslim, nationalist, and communist agitation against the Dutch; with captured Japanese arms, Indonesia could resist reimposition of Dutch authority. After World War II the Dutch tried to regain some of their lost control in Indonesia. The Sukarno regime held fast through three years of intermittent war, however, and the Dutch found no allies and no international support. In 1950 Indonesia became a centralized, independent republic.

Decolonization continued across the region in the years after World War II. Japan's defeat led to a seven-year occupation by the United States. The first colonial war was in Indochina, where a power vacuum, caused by Japan's removal after wartime occupation, gave a unique opportunity to the communist Viet Minh. When in 1946 the French Army tried to regain the colony, the communists, proclaiming a republic, resorted to the political and military strategies of Mao Tse-tung to wear down and eventually defeat France. All chances for maintaining a semi-colonial administration in Indochina ended when the communists won the civil war in China (1949). Eventually, in 1954, when the French engaged the communist armies in a pitched battle at Dien Bien Phu, the communists won with the help of new heavy guns supplied by the Chinese. The Fourth Republic left Indochina under the terms of the Geneva Accords (1954), which set up two independent regimes. Likewise, the Philippines and Burma became independent in 1946 and 1948, respectively; Malaysia gained independence in 1957 but remained a member of the British Commonwealth.

CHAPTER ONE

JAPAN

T he seclusion of Japan ended in 1853 with the arrival of a United States naval fleet commanded by Cmdre. Matthew C. Perry. He had been instructed to open Japan to foreign trade and diplomatic contact. The Edo *bakufu* (shogunate), recognizing U.S. military superiority, signed a treaty of friendship with the United States during a second visit by Perry in 1854.

The Netherlands, Russia, Great Britain, and France followed the lead of the United States. By 1859 the *bakufu* had been pressured into signing a series of "unequal treaties" opening several Japanese ports to foreign trade. These treaties were called unequal because they gave privileges to Western powers at Japan's expense. Western nationals were given the right of extraterritoriality, or exemption from local law. Tariff rates were established that the Japanese government could not alter.

Many Japanese regarded the surrender to the West as a national humiliation, and the *bakufu*'s authority declined rapidly. There were growing demands for the expulsion of the foreigners and for the restoration of political power to the emperor. These demands were supported by the court and two powerful daimyo (a social class of powerful landowners) domains in western Japan—Satsuma (in southern Kyushu) and Choshu (in extreme western Honshu). In 1868 the Tokugawa shogun was forced to give up power. A new government was established under the young emperor Mutsuhito, who took the reign name of Meiji ("enlightened government"). This transfer of power from the Tokugawa shogunate to the Meiji emperor, known as the Meiji Restoration, is regarded as the beginning of Japan's modern era.

THE MEIJI RESTORATION

Leaders of the new government were former samurai of Satsuma and Choshu, such as Okubo Toshimichi, Kido Takayoshi, and Saigo Takamori. They wished to end the "unequal treaties" and to catch up militarily with the Western countries. Their first task, however, was to create internal order. A centralized administration replaced the daimyo system, many class distinctions were abolished, and a conscript army was built up, replacing the samurai, or warrior class. In 1868 Edo was renamed Tokyo, meaning "eastern capital," and designated the new imperial capital.

During the 1870s the army quelled a number of rebellions by former samurai who objected to rapid modernization. This included the ill-fated Satsuma rebellion of 1877, led by Saigo, who had resigned from the government in 1873. This rebellion was the last major challenge to the new regime.

The imperial government also laid the foundations for an industrial economy. Modern money and banking systems were introduced. Railroads, telegraph and telephone lines, and factories were built, using the newest technology. The government funded private enterprises, and new laws permitted the private ownership of land. Leaders such as Mori Arinori helped create a modern educational system. Compulsory universal education was instituted in 1872. By 1905 nearly 95 percent of Japanese school-age children were in school, and Japan soon achieved one of the highest literacy rates in the world.

A constitution was drafted in the 1880s under the direction of the political leader Ito Hirobumi. He took as his model the institutions of the German empire. The constitution, finally put into force in 1889, gave strong executive powers to the emperor and a privy council. A prime minister headed a cabinet whose members were individually responsible to the emperor. Legislative powers were exercised by a two-house parliament, or Diet. The upper house, the House of Peers, consisted mainly of a new nobility created in 1884. The lower house, the House of Representatives, was elected by male taxpayers over 25 years of age.

By the 1890s Japan's rapid modernization had made it the most powerful country in Asia. Extraterritoriality was relinquished by Great Britain, the United States, and the other Western powers by 1899. But Meiji leaders such as Ito and Yamagata Aritomo remained suspicious of Western imperialism. Using its growing economic and military power, Japan sought to build an empire of its own.

Treaty reform, designed to end the foreigners' judicial and economic privileges provided by extraterritoriality and fixed customs duties, was sought as early as 1871 when the Iwakura mission went to the United States and Europe. The Western powers insisted, however, that they could not revise the treaties until Japanese legal institutions were reformed along European and American lines. Efforts to reach a compromise settlement in the 1880s were rejected by the press and opposition groups in Japan. It was not until 1894, therefore, that treaty provisions for extraterritoriality were formally changed.

During the first half of the Meiji period, Asian relations were seen as less important than domestic development. In 1874 a punitive expedition was launched against Formosa (Taiwan) to chastise the aborigines for murdering Ryukyuan fishermen. This lent support to Japanese claims to the Ryukyu Islands, which had been under Satsuma influence in Tokugawa times. Despite Chinese protests, the Ryukyus were incorporated into Japan in 1879.

Meanwhile, calls for an aggressive foreign policy in Korea, aired by Japanese nationalists and some liberals, were steadily rejected by the Meiji leaders. At the same time, China became increasingly concerned about expanding Japanese influence in Korea, which China still viewed as a tributary state. Incidents on the peninsula in 1882 and 1884 that might have involved China and Japan in war were settled by compromise, and in 1885 China and Japan agreed that neither would send troops to Korea without first informing the other.

THE SINO-JAPANESE WAR

By the early 1890s Chinese influence in Korea had increased. In 1894 Korea requested Chinese assistance in putting down a local rebellion. When the Chinese notified Tokyo of this, Japan quickly rushed troops to Korea. With the rebellion crushed, neither side withdrew. The Sino-Japanese War formally erupted in July 1894. Japanese forces proved to be superior on both land and sea, and, with the loss of its northern fleet, China sued for peace. The peace treaty negotiated at Shimonoseki was formally signed on April 17, 1895; both sides recognized the independence of Korea, and China ceded to Japan Formosa, the Pescadores Islands, and the Liaodong Peninsula, granted Japan all rights enjoyed by European powers, and made significant economic concessions, including the opening of new treaty ports and a large indemnity in gold. A commercial treaty giving Japan special tax exemptions and other trade and manufacturing privileges was signed in 1896. Japan thus marked its own emancipation from the unequal treaties by imposing even harsher terms on its neighbour.

Meanwhile, France, Russia, and Germany were not willing to endorse Japanese gains and forced the return of the Liaodong Peninsula to China. Insult was added to injury when Russia leased the same territory with its important naval base, Port Arthur (now Lü-shun), from China in 1898. The war thus demonstrated that the Japanese could not maintain Asian military victories without Western sufferance. At the same time, it proved a tremendous source of prestige for Japan and brought the government much internal support; it also strengthened the hand of the military in national affairs.

THE RUSSO-JAPANESE WAR

Reluctant to accept Japanese leadership, Korea instead sought Russia's help. During the Boxer Rebellion (1900) in China, Japanese troops played a major part in the allied expedition to rescue foreign nationals in Beijing, but Russia occupied southern Manchuria, thereby strengthening its links with Korea. Realizing the need for protection against multiple European enemies, the Japanese began talks with England that led to the Anglo-Japanese Alliance (1902). In this pact both countries agreed to aid the other in the event of an attack by two or more powers but remain neutral if the other went to war with a single enemy. Backed by Britain, Tokyo was prepared to take a firmer stand against Russian advances in Manchuria and Korea.

In 1904 Japanese ships attacked the Russian fleet at Port Arthur without warning. In the Russo-Japanese War (1904–05) that followed, Japanese arms were everywhere successful; the most spectacular victory occurred in the Tsushima Strait, where the ships of Admiral Tōgō Heihachirō destroyed the Russian Baltic fleet. But the war was extremely costly in Japanese lives and treasure, and Japan was relieved when U.S. President Theodore Roosevelt offered to mediate a peace settlement. The Treaty of Portsmouth, signed on Sept. 5, 1905, gave Japan primacy in Korea, and Russia granted to Japan its economic and political interests in southern Manchuria, including the Liaodong Peninsula. Russia also ceded to Japan the southern half of the island of Sakhalin. The victory over Russia altered the balance of power in East Asia, and it encouraged nationalist movements in India and the Middle East. But at home Japan's failure to gain an indemnity to pay for the heavy war costs made the treaty unpopular.

A Japanese warship fights in the Russo-Japanese War in 1904, off the coast of the Liaodong Peninsula, in Liaoning, China.

JAPANESE EXPANSIONISM

After the conclusion of the war, Japanese leaders gained a free hand in Korea. Korean opposition to Japanese "reforms" was no longer tolerated. Itō Hirobumi, sent to Korea as resident general, forced through treaties that gave Korea little more than protectorate status and ordered the abdication of the Korean king. Itō's assassination in 1909 led to Korea's annexation by Japan the following year. Korean liberties and resistance were crushed. By 1912, when the Meiji emperor died, Japan had not only achieved equality with the West but also had become the strongest imperialist power in East Asia.

Japan had abundant opportunity to use its new power in the years that followed. During World War I it fought on the Allied side but limited its activities to seizing German possessions in China and the Pacific. When China sought the return of former German holdings in Shantung province, Japan responded with the so-called Twenty-one Demands, issued in 1915, that tried to pressure China into widespread concessions ranging from extended leases in Manchuria and joint control of China's coal and iron resources to policy matters regarding harbours and the policing of Chinese cities. While giving in on a number of specific issues, the Chinese resisted the most

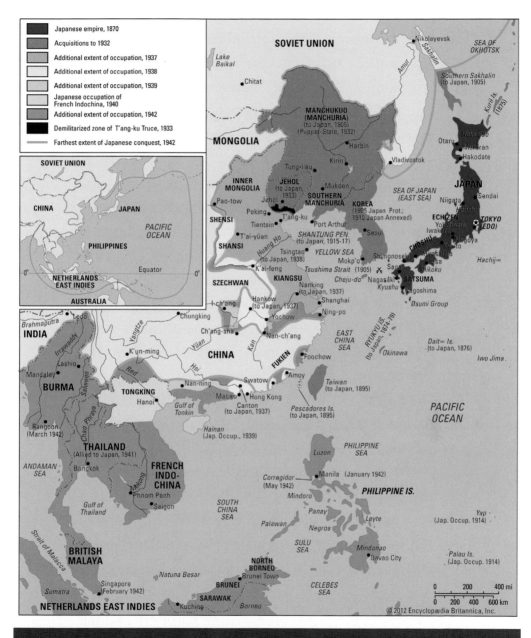

Japanese empire, 1870
Acquisitions to 1932
Additional extent of occupation, 1937
Additional extent of occupation, 1938
Additional extent of occupation, 1939
Japanese occupation of French Indochina, 1940
Additional extent of occupation, 1942
Demilitarized zone of T'ang-ku Truce, 1933
Farthest extent of Japanese conquest, 1942

Japanese expansion in the late 19th and early 20th centuries stretched west into China, south to Indonesia, and across mainland Southeast Asia.

extreme Japanese demands that would have turned China into a Japanese ward. Despite its economic gains, Japan's World War I China policy left behind a legacy of ill feeling and distrust, both in China and in the West. The greediness of Japanese demands and China's chagrin at its failure to recover its losses in the Treaty of Versailles (1919) cost Japan any hope of Chinese friendship. Subsequent Japanese sponsorship of corrupt warlord regimes in Manchuria and North China helped to confirm the anti-Japanese nature of modern Chinese nationalism.

The part played by Japan in the Allied intervention in Siberia following the Bolshevik Revolution of 1918 caused further concerns about Japanese expansion. One of the principal reasons for the disarmament conference held in Washington, D.C., in 1921–22, was to reduce Japanese influence. A network of treaties was designed to place restraints on Japanese ambitions while guaranteeing Japanese security. These treaties included a Four-Power Pact, between Japan, Great Britain, the United States, and France, that replaced the Anglo-Japanese Alliance, and a Five-Power Naval Limitation Treaty (with Italy) that set limits for battleships at a ratio of five for Great Britain and the United States to three for Japan. An agreement on the fortification of Pacific island bases was intended to assure Japan of security in its home waters. Finally a Nine-Power Pact would, it was hoped, protect China from further unilateral demands. Japan subsequently agreed to retire from Shantung, and, shortly thereafter, Japanese armies withdrew from Siberia and northern Sakhalin. In 1925 a treaty with the Soviet Union extended recognition to the U.S.S.R. and ended active hostilities.

Thus, by the mid-1920s Japan's great surge forward in Asia and the Pacific had ended. This brought hope that a new quality of moderation and reasonableness, based on the absence of irritating reminders of inferiority and weakness, might characterize Japanese policy.

THE RISE OF THE MILITARISTS

The notion that expansion through military conquest would solve Japan's economic problems gained currency during the Great Depression of the 1930s. It was argued that the rapid growth of Japan's population—which stood at close to 65 million in 1930—necessitated large food imports. To sustain such imports, Japan had to be able to export. Western tariffs limited exports, while discriminatory legislation in many countries and anti-Japanese racism served as barriers to emigration. Chinese and Japanese efforts to secure racial equality in the League of Nations covenant had been rejected by Western statesmen. Thus, it was argued, Japan had no recourse but to use force.

To these economic and racial arguments was added the military's distrust of party government. The Washington Conference had allowed a smaller ratio of naval strength than the navy desired, while the government of Prime Minister Hamaguchi Osachi in 1930 had accepted the London Naval Conference's limits on heavy cruisers over military objections. In 1925 Katō Takaaki had cut the army by four divisions. Many military men objected to the restraint shown by Japan toward the Chinese Nationalists' northern expedition of 1926 and 1927 and wanted Japan to take a harder line in China. Under Prime Minister Tanaka Giichi the Seiyūkai cabinet reversed earlier policy by intervening in Shantung in 1927 and 1928. But Tanaka was replaced by Hamaguchi in 1929, and under his cabinet the policy of moderation was restored. The army and its supporters felt that such vacillation earned Japan ill will and boycotts in China without gaining any advantages.

While many military leaders chafed under the restrictions that civilian governments placed upon them, they still retained considerable power. It would be wrong to attribute such resentment to all, or even most, of the high command, but enough army officers held such views to become a locus for dissatisfaction among other groups in Japanese society. The idea of the frugal and selfless samurai served as a useful contrast to the stock portrait of the selfish party politician.

Economic pressures and political misgivings were further exploited by civilian ultranationalists who portrayed parliamentary government as being "un-Japanese." A number of rightist organizations existed that were dedicated to the theme of internal purity and external expansion. These sought to preserve what they thought was unique in the Japanese spirit and fought against excessive Western influence. Some originated in the Meiji period, when nationalists had felt obliged to work for a "fundamental settlement" of differences with Russia. Most, like the Black Dragon Society (Kokuryūkai), combined continental adventurism and a strong nationalist stance with opposition to party government, big business, acculturation, and Westernization. By allying with other rightists, they alternately terrorized and intimidated their presumed opponents. A number of business leaders and political figures were killed, and the assassins' success in publicizing and dramatizing the virtues they claimed to embody had a considerable impact on the troubled 1930s. It is clear, however, that the terrorists never had as much influence as they claimed or as the West believed.

The principal force against parliamentary government was provided by junior military officers, who were largely from rural backgrounds. Distrustful of their senior leaders, ignorant of political economy, and contemptuous of the urban luxuries of politicians, such officers were ready marks for rightist theorists. Many of them had goals that were national-socialist in character. Kita Ikki, a former socialist and one-time member of the Black Dragon Society, contended that the Meiji constitution should be suspended in favour of a revolutionary regime advised by "national patriots" and headed by a military government, which should nationalize large properties, limit wealth, end party government and the peerage, and prepare to take the leadership of a revolutionary Asia. Kita helped persuade a number of young officers to take part in the violence of the 1930s with the hope of achieving these ends.

AGGRESSION IN MANCHURIA

The Kwantung Army, which occupied the Kwantung (Liaodong) Peninsula and patrolled the South Manchurian Railway zone, included officers who were keenly aware of Japan's continental interests and were prepared to take steps to further them. They hoped to place the civilian government in an untenable position and to force its hand. The Tokyo terrorists similarly sought to change foreign as well as domestic policies. The pattern of direct action in Manchuria began with the murder in 1928 of Chang Tso-lin, the warlord ruler of Manchuria. The action, though not authorized by the Tanaka government, helped bring about its fall. Neither the cabinet nor the Diet dared to investigate and punish those responsible. This convinced extremist officers that their lofty motives would make retribution impossible. The succeeding government of Prime Minister Hamaguchi sought to curtail military activists and their powers. The next plots, therefore, were aimed at replacing civilian rule, and Hamaguchi was mortally wounded by an assassin in 1930. In March 1931 a coup involving highly placed army generals was planned but abandoned.

On Sept. 18, 1931, came the Mukden (or Manchurian) Incident, which launched Japanese aggression in East Asia. A Kwantung Army charge that Chinese soldiers had tried to bomb a South Manchurian Railway train (which arrived at its destination safely) resulted in a speedy and unauthorized capture of Mukden (now Shen-yang), followed by the occupation of all Manchuria. The civilian government in Tokyo could not stop the army, and even army headquarters was not always in full control of the field commanders. Prime Minister Wakatsuki Reijirō gave way in December 1931 to Inukai Tsuy-

Japanese troops invaded Manchuria in 1931. Over the next decade, imperial Japan emerged as a threat to East Asia, Southeast Asia, the Pacific, and beyond.

oshi. Inukai's plans to stop the army by imperial intervention were frustrated.

On May 15, 1932, naval officers took the lead in a terrorist attack in Tokyo that cost Inukai his life but failed to secure a proclamation of martial law. The army now announced that it would accept no party cabinet. To forestall its desire for power, the last *genrō*, Saionji, suggested retired Admiral Saitō Makoto as prime minister. Plotting continued, culminating in a revolt of a regiment about to leave for Manchuria. On Feb. 26, 1936, several outstanding statesmen (including Saitō) were murdered; Prime Minister Okada Keisuke escaped when the assassins mistakenly shot his brother-in-law. For more than three days the rebel units held much of downtown Tokyo. When the revolt was put down on February 29, the ringleaders were quickly arrested and executed. Within the army, the influence of the young extremists now gave way to more conservative officers and generals who were less concerned with domestic reform, while sharing many of the foreign-policy goals of the young fanatics.

The only possible source of prestige sufficient to thwart the military lay with the throne. But the senior statesmen were cautious lest they imperil the imperial institution itself. The young emperor Hirohito had been enthroned in 1926, taking as his reign name Shōwa ("Enlightened Peace"). His outlook was more progressive than that of his predecessors; he had traveled in the West, and his interests lay in marine biology. Those close to the throne feared that a strong stand by the emperor would only widen the search for victims and could lead to his dethronement. As international criticism of Japan's aggression grew, many Japanese rallied to support the army.

THE ROAD TO WORLD WAR II

Each advance by the military extremists gained them new concessions from the moderate elements in the government and brought greater foreign hostility and distrust. Rather than oppose the military, the government agreed to reconstitute Manchuria as an "independent" state, Manchukuo. The last Manchu emperor of China, P'u-i, was declared regent and later enthroned as emperor in 1934. Actual control lay with the Kwantung Army, however; all key positions were held by Japanese, with surface authority vested in cooperative Chinese and Manchu. A League of Nations committee recommended in October 1932 that Japanese troops be withdrawn, Chinese sovereignty restored, and a large measure of autonomy granted to

Manchuria. The League called upon member states to withhold recognition from the new puppet state. Japan's response was to formally withdraw from the world body in 1933. Thereafter, Japan poured technicians and capital into Manchukuo, exploiting its rich resources to establish the base for the heavy-industry complex that was to undergird its "new order" in East Asia.

In northern China, boundary areas were consolidated in order to enlarge Japan's economic sphere. In early 1932 the Japanese navy precipitated an incident at Shanghai in order to end a boycott of Japanese goods; but Japan was not yet prepared to challenge other powers for control of central China, and a League of Nations commission arranged terms for a withdrawal. By 1934, however, Japan had made it clear that it would brook no interference in its China policy and that Chinese attempts to procure technical or military assistance elsewhere would bring Japanese opposition.

Further external ambitions had to wait, however, for the resolution of domestic crises. The military revolt in Tokyo in February 1936 marked the high point of extremist action. In its wake power shifted to the military conservatives. Moreover, the finance minister Takahashi Korekiyo, whose policies had brought Japan out of its economic depression, was killed, and his opposition to further inflationary spending was thus stilled. In politics, the confrontation between the parties and the army continued. Efforts to find a leader who could represent both military and civilian interests led to the appointment to the premiership of the popular but ineffective Konoe Fumimaro, scion of an ancient court family, in 1937. Meanwhile, in China the Nationalist leader Chiang Kai-shek had been kidnapped in the Sian Incident in December 1936, and this led to an anti-Japanese united front by Nationalists and communists.

Domestic politics revealed, moreover, that the Japanese people were not yet prepared to renounce their parliamentary system. In the spring of 1937, general elections showed startling gains for the new Social Mass (or Social Masses) Party (Shakai Taishūtō), which received 36 out of 466 seats, and a heavy majority of the remainder went to the Seiyūkai and Minseitō, which had combined forces against the government and its policies. The time seemed ready for new efforts by civilian leaders, but in the field the armies preempted them.

On July 7, 1937, Japanese troops engaged Chinese units at the Marco Polo Bridge near Beijing, leading to warfare between China and Japan. Japanese armies took Nanking, Han-k'ou (Hankow), and Canton despite vigorous Chinese resistance; Nanking was brutally pillaged by Japanese troops. To the north, Inner Mongolia and China's northern provinces were invaded. On discovering that the Nationalist government, which had retreated up the Yangtze to Chungking, refused to compromise, the Japanese installed a more cooperative regime at Nanking in 1940.

In November 1936 Japan signed the Anti-Comintern Pact with Germany and later with Italy. This was replaced by the Tripartite Pact in September 1940, which recognized Japan as the leader of a new order in Asia; Japan, Germany, and Italy agreed to assist each other if they were attacked by any additional power not yet at war with them. The intended target was the United States, since the Soviets and Nazis had already signed a nonaggression pact in 1939, and the Soviets were invited to join the new agreement later in 1940.

Japanese relations with the Soviet Union were considerably less cordial than those with Germany. The Soviets consented, however, to sell the Chinese Eastern Railway to the South Manchurian Railway in 1935, thereby strengthening Manchukuo. In 1937 the Soviet Union signed a nonaggression pact with China, and in 1938 and 1939 Soviet and Japanese armies tested each other in two full-scale battles along the border of Manchukuo. But in April 1941 a neutrality pact was signed with the Soviet Union, with Germany acting as intermediary.

Japanese-German ties were never close or effective. Both parties were limited in their cooperation by distance, distrust, and claims of racial superiority. The Japanese were uninformed about Nazi plans for attacking the Soviet Union, and the Germans were not told of Japan's plans to attack Pearl Harbor in Hawaii. Nor, despite formal statements of rapport, did Japan's state structure approach the totalitarianism of the Nazis. A national-mobilization law (1938) gave the Konoe government sweeping economic and political powers, and in 1940, under the second Konoe cabinet, the Imperial Rule Assistance Association was established to merge the political parties into one central organization; yet, the institutional structure of the Meiji constitution was never altered, and the wartime governments never achieved full control over interservice competition. The Imperial Rule Assistance Association failed to mobilize all segments of national life around a leader. The emperor remained a symbol, albeit an increasingly military one, and no führer could compete without endangering the national polity. Wartime social and economic thought retained important vestiges of an agrarianism and familism that were in essence premodern rather than totalitarian.

Japan's relations with the democratic powers deteriorated steadily. The United States and Great Britain did what they could to assist the Chinese Nationalist cause. The Burma Road into southern China permitted the transport of minimal supplies to Nationalist forces. Constant Japanese efforts to close this route led to further tensions between Great Britain and Japan. Anti-Japanese feeling strengthened in the United States, especially after the sinking of a U.S. gunboat in the Yangtze River in 1937. In 1939 U.S. Secretary of State Cordell Hull renounced the 1911 treaty of commerce with Japan, and thus embargoes became possible in 1940. President Franklin Roosevelt's efforts to rally public opinion against aggressors included efforts to stop Japan, but, even after war broke out in Europe in 1939, American public opinion rejected involvement abroad.

WORLD WAR II AND DEFEAT

The European war presented the Japanese with tempting opportunities. After the Nazi attack on Russia in 1941, the Japanese were torn between German urgings to join the war against the Soviets and their natural inclination to seek richer prizes from the European colonial territories to the south. In 1940 Japan occupied northern Indochina in an attempt to block access to supplies for the Chinese Nationalists, and in July 1941 it announced a joint protectorate with Vichy France over the whole colony. This opened the way for further moves into Southeast Asia.

The United States reacted to the occupation of Indochina by freezing Japanese assets and embargoing oil. The Japanese now faced the choices of either

The Japanese Imperial Army invaded French Indochina in September 1940. Three months earlier, France had fallen to Germany, Japan's ally.

withdrawing from Indochina, and possibly China, or seizing the sources of oil production in the Dutch East Indies. Negotiations with Washington were initiated by the second Konoe cabinet. Konoe was willing to withdraw from Indochina, and he sought a personal meeting with Roosevelt, hoping that any U.S. concessions or favours would strengthen his hand against the military. But the State Department refused to agree to such a meeting without prior Japanese concessions. Having failed in his negotiations, Konoe resigned in October 1941 and was immediately succeeded by his war minister, General Tōjō Hideki. Meanwhile, Secretary of State Hull rejected Japan's "final offer": Japan would withdraw from Indochina after China had come to terms in return for U.S. promises to resume oil shipments, cease aid to China, and unfreeze Japanese assets.

With Japan's decision for war made, the negotiators received instructions to continue to negotiate, but preparations for the opening strike against the U.S. fleet at Pearl Harbor were already in motion. Japan's war aims were to establish a "new order in East Asia," built on a "coprosperity" concept that placed Japan at the centre of an economic bloc consisting of Manchuria, Korea, and North China that would draw on the raw materials of the rich colonies of Southeast Asia, while inspiring these to friendship and alliance by destroying their previous masters. In practice, "East Asia for the Asiatics," the slogan that headed the campaign, came to mean "East Asia for Japan."

The attack on Pearl Harbor (Dec. 7 [Dec. 8 in Japan], 1941) achieved complete surprise and success. It also unified American opinion and determination to see the war through to a successful conclusion. The Japanese had expected that, once they fortified their new holdings, a reconquest would be so expensive in lives and treasure that it would discourage the "soft" democracies. Instead, the U.S. fleet was rebuilt with astonishing speed, and the chain of defenses was breached before the riches of the newly conquered territories could be effectively tapped by Japan.

The first years of the war brought Japan great success. In the Philippines, Japanese troops occupied Manila in January 1942, although Corregidor held out until May; Singapore fell in February, and the Dutch East Indies and Rangoon (Burma) in early March. The Allies had difficulty maintaining communications with Australia, and British naval losses promised the Japanese navy further freedom of action. Tōjō grew in confidence and popularity and began to style himself somewhat in the manner of a fascist leader. But the U.S. Navy had not been permanently driven from the South Pacific. The Battle of Midway in June 1942 cost the Japanese fleet four aircraft carriers and many seasoned pilots, and the battle for Guadalcanal Island in the Solomons ended with Japanese withdrawal in February 1943.

After Midway, Japanese naval leaders secretly concluded that Japan's outlook for victory was poor. When the fall of Saipan in July 1944 brought U.S. bombers within range of Tokyo, the Tōjō cabinet was replaced by that of Koiso Kuniaki. Koiso formed a supreme war-direction council designed to link the cabinet and the high command. Many in government realized that the war was lost, but none had a program for ending the war that was acceptable to the military. There were also grave problems in breaking the news to the Japanese people, who had been told only of victories. Great firebombing raids in 1945 brought destruction to every major city except the old capital of Kyōto; but the generals were bent on continuing the war, confident that a major victory or protracted battle would help gain honourable terms. The Allied talk of unconditional surrender provided a good excuse to continue the fight.

In February 1945 the emperor met with a group of senior statesmen to discuss steps that might be taken. When U.S. landings were made on Okinawa in April, the Koiso government fell. The problem of the new premier, Admiral Suzuki Kantarō, was not whether to end the war but how best to do it. The first plan advanced was to ask the Soviet Union, which was still at peace with Japan, to intercede with the Allies. The Soviet government had agreed, however, to enter the war; consequently, its reply was delayed while Soviet leaders participated in the Potsdam Conference in July. The Potsdam Declaration issued on July 26 offered the first ray of hope with its statement that Japan would not be "enslaved as a race, nor destroyed as a nation."

Atomic bombs largely destroyed the cities of Hiroshima and Nagasaki on August 6 and 9, respectively. On August 8 the Soviet Union declared war and the next day marched into Manchuria, where the Kwantung Army could offer only token resistance. The Japanese government attempted to gain as its sole condition for surrender a qualification for the preservation of the imperial institution; after the Allies agreed to respect the will of the Japanese people, the emperor insisted on surrender. The Pacific war came to an end on August 14 (August 15 in Japan). The formal surrender was signed on September 2 in Tokyo Bay aboard the battleship USS *Missouri*.

Military extremists attempted unsuccessfully to prevent the radio broadcast of the emperor's announcement to the nation. There were a number of suicides among the military officers and nationalists who felt themselves dishonoured, but the emperor's prestige and personal will, once expressed, sufficed to bring an orderly transition. To increase the appearance of direct rule, the Suzuki cabinet was replaced by that of Prince Higashikuni Naruhiko.

Postwar investigators concluded that neither the atomic bombs nor the Soviet entry into the war was central to the decision to surrender, although they probably helped to advance the date. It was determined that submarine blockade of the Japanese islands had brought economic defeat by preventing exploitation of Japan's new colonies, sinking merchant tonnage, and convincing Japanese leaders of the hopelessness of the war. Bombing brought the consciousness of defeat to the people. The destruction of the Japanese navy and air force jeopardized the home islands. Japan's largest armies, however, were never defeated, and this was responsible for the army's eagerness to fight on.

By the end of the war, Japan's cities were destroyed, its stockpiles exhausted, and its industrial capacity gutted. The government stood without prestige or respect. An alarming shortage of food and rising inflation threatened what remained of national strength.

POSTWAR OCCUPATION

From 1945 to 1952 Japan was under Allied military occupation, headed by the Supreme Commander for Allied Powers (SCAP), a position held by U.S. Gen. Douglas MacArthur until 1951. Although nominally directed by a multinational Far Eastern Commission in Washington, D.C., and an Allied Council in Tokyo—which included the United States, the Soviet Union, China, and the Commonwealth countries—the occupation was almost entirely an American affair. While MacArthur developed a large General Headquarters in Tokyo to carry out occupation policy, supported by local "military government" teams, Japan, unlike Germany, was not governed directly by foreign troops. Instead, SCAP relied on the Japanese government and its organs, particularly the bureaucracy, to carry out its directives.

The occupation, like the Taika Reform of the 7th century and the Meiji Restoration 80 years earlier, represented a period of rapid social and institutional change that was based on the borrowing and incorporation of foreign models. General principles for the proposed governance of Japan had been spelled out in the Potsdam Declaration and elucidated in U.S. government policy statements drawn up and forwarded to MacArthur in August 1945. The essence of these policies was simple and straightforward: the demilitarization of Japan, so that it would not again become a danger to peace; democratization, meaning that, while no particular form of government would be forced upon the Japanese, efforts would be made to develop a political system under which individual rights would be guaranteed and protected; and the establishment of an economy that could adequately support a peaceful and democratic Japan.

MacArthur himself shared the vision of a demilitarized and democratic Japan and was well suited to the task at hand. An administrator of considerable skill, he possessed elements of leadership and charisma that appealed to the defeated Japanese. Brooking neither domestic nor foreign interference, MacArthur enthusiastically set about creating a new Japan. He encouraged an environment in which new forces could and did rise, and, where his reforms corresponded to trends already established in Japanese society, they played a vital role in Japan's recovery as a free and independent nation.

In the early months of the occupation, SCAP acted swiftly to remove the principal supports of the militarist state. The armed forces were demobilized and millions of Japanese troops and civilians abroad repatriated. The empire was disbanded. State Shintō was disestablished, and nationalist organizations were abolished and their members removed from important posts. Japan's armament industries were dismantled. The Home Ministry with its prewar powers over the police and local government was abolished; the police force was decentralized and its extensive power revoked. The Education Ministry's sweeping powers over education were curtailed, and compulsory courses on ethics (*shūshin*) were eliminated. All individuals prominent in wartime organizations and politics, including commissioned officers of the armed services and all high executives of the principal industrial firms, were removed from their positions. An international tribunal was established to conduct war crimes trials, and seven men, including the wartime prime minister Tōjō, were convicted and hanged; another 16 were sentenced to life imprisonment.

The most important reform carried out by the occupation was the establishment of a new constitution. In 1945 SCAP made it clear to Japanese government leaders that revision of the Meiji constitution should receive their highest priority. When Japanese efforts to write a new document proved inadequate, MacArthur's government section prepared its own draft and presented it to the Japanese government as a basis for further deliberations. Endorsed by the emperor, this document was placed before the first postwar Diet in April 1946. It was formally promulgated on November 3 and went into effect on May 3, 1947.

The emphasis in the new constitution was clearly on the people rather than the throne. Sovereignty now lay with the people. A 31-article bill of rights followed, with Article 9 renouncing forever "war as a sovereign right of the nation" and pledging that "land, sea and air forces" would "never be maintained." The emperor, no longer "sacred" or "inviolable," was now described as the "symbol of the state and of the unity of the people." The constitution called for a bicameral Diet, with the greatest power concentrated in the House of Representatives, members of which would now be elected by both men and women. The old peerage was dissolved, and the House of Peers was replaced by a House of Councillors. The Privy Council was abolished. The prime minister was to be chosen by the Diet from its members, and an independent judiciary was established with the right of judicial review.

Despite its hasty preparation and foreign inspiration, the new constitution gained wide public support. Although the ruling conservatives desired to revise it after Japan regained its sovereignty in 1952, and an official commission favoured changes in the constitution in 1964, no political group in postwar

Japan has been able to secure the two-thirds majority needed to make revisions. While parts of the structure established by the document have been modified through administrative actions—including a reversal of the principle of decentralization in areas such as the police, the school system, and some spheres of local administration—and while Article 9 has been compromised by the decision to form a National Police Reserve that in 1954 became the Self-Defense Forces, the basic principles of the constitution have enjoyed support among all factions in Japanese politics. Executive leadership proved to be the chief asset of the new institutions, and, with the abolition of the competing forces that had hampered the premiers of the 1930s, Japan's postwar prime ministers have found themselves firmly in charge of the administration and (with limited rearmament) the armed forces as well. Thus, responsible leadership gradually replaced the ambiguous claims of imperial rule of earlier days.

Politics under the occupation and new constitution experienced considerable flux, as many of Japan's prewar leaders found themselves purged from public office and the two prewar parties, the Seiyūkai and Minseitō, restructured themselves as the Liberal and Progressive parties, respectively (the latter eventually becoming the Japan Democratic

ECONOMIC AND SOCIAL CHANGES IN OCCUPIED JAPAN

The occupation's political democratization was reinforced by economic and social changes. SCAP was aware that political democracy in Japan required not only a weakening of the value structure of the hierarchic "family state," which restricted the individual, but also a liberation of the Japanese people from the economic forces that reinforced such a state. With nearly half of Japan's farmers subsisting as tenants, Americans saw little hope for democracy in Japan without significant changes in the ownership of land. Occupation authorities therefore set out to establish a program of land reform that was designed to convert tenants into owner-farmers. Through legislation a plan was devised whereby landlords, many of whom lived in the cities, were forced to divest themselves of a high proportion of their holdings to the government. This land was then sold to tenants on favourable terms. Given the fact that prices were set at wartime and postwar pre-inflation rates, landlords were essentially

(CONTINUED ON THE NEXT PAGE)

(CONTINUED FROM THE PREVIOUS PAGE)

expropriated. Still, the reforms were implemented with great efficiency and in the end proved highly successful.

Supported by favourable tax and price arrangements, the majority of Japan's new owner-farmers gained control of their land, which on average consisted of about 2.5 acres (1 hectare) per farm. Benefited by agricultural subsidies and government-maintained high agricultural prices, the Japanese countryside experienced increased prosperity. Rural voters became not only the mainstay of the conservative Liberal-Democratic Party (LDP) after its formation in 1955 (fulfilling the original American intent), but as one of Japan's most powerful lobbies they often successfully resisted agricultural trade liberalization. In a reversal of the Taishō dilemma that sprang from low domestic consumption, land reform and agricultural price supports contributed significantly to Japan's emergence as a consumer economy in the 1950s and '60s.

Initial Allied plans had contemplated exacting heavy reparations from Japan, but the unsettled state of other Asian countries that were to have been recipients brought reconsideration. Except for Japanese assets overseas and a small number of war plants, reparations were largely limited to those worked out between Japan and its Asian victims after the Treaty of Peace with Japan was signed in 1951.

Strengthening the influence of labour in Japan also was seen as important for the advancement of democracy. A new Ministry of Labour was established in 1947. Laws on trade unions and labour relations modeled on New Deal legislation in the United States were passed, and a strong union movement was initially encouraged. Leaders of this movement included a number of socialists and communists who had been released from prison by the occupation. But a proposed general strike in 1947 and the Cold War-induced shift toward rapid economic reconstruction, anti-inflationary policies, and a control of radicalism quickly resulted in a purge of left-wing labour leaders and an effort to bring labour under government control. In 1948 SCAP ordered the government to take steps to deprive government workers—including those in communications unions—of the right to strike. At the same time a new labour organization, the General Council of Trade Unions of Japan (Sōhyō), was sponsored as a counterweight and gradual replacement for

(CONTINUED ON THE NEXT PAGE)

(CONTINUED FROM THE PREVIOUS PAGE)

the Congress of Industrial Labour Unions of Japan (Sambetsu Kaigi), which had become dominated by the left. In the late 1950s Sōhyō, too, had become increasingly antigovernment and anti-American, its Marxist and socialist orientation finding a political voice in the Japan Socialist Party (JSP), of which it became the leading supporter.

Postwar social legislation also provided relief from earlier restrictions. The civil code, which had supported the power of the male family head in the past, was rewritten to allow for equality between the sexes and joint inheritance rights. Women were given the right to vote and to sit in the Diet.

Party). On the left wing, the socialists and communists also reorganized their respective parties. Initial postwar elections included many political splinter groups. Faced with a lack of consensus, cabinets tended to be unstable and short-lived. This was true of the first Yoshida Shigeru cabinet (1946–47), which implemented most of the early SCAP reforms only to be replaced by an equally transitory cabinet headed by the Socialist Katayama Tetsu (1947–48).

A similar fate confronted Ashida Hitoshi, who became prime minister for five months in 1948. Yoshida's return to power in the fall of 1948 resulted in a more stable situation and ushered in the Yoshida era, which lasted until 1954.

During those years, Japan capitalized on the economic benefits of close cooperation with the United States during the Korean War (1950–53), which laid the groundwork for national reconstruction and for the essential postwar U.S.-Japan relationship. In 1951 Yoshida achieved what he regarded as his greatest accomplishment—the restoration of national sovereignty—by taking Japan to the San Francisco peace conference. There, with the American negotiator John Foster Dulles and representatives of 47 nations, he hammered out the final details of the Treaty of Peace with Japan. The treaty was formally signed on Sept. 8, 1951, and the occupation of Japan ended on April 28, 1952.

THE ERA OF RAPID GROWTH

From 1952 to 1973 Japan experienced accelerated economic growth and social change. By 1952 Japan had at last regained its prewar industrial output. Thereafter, the economy expanded at unprecedented rates. At the same time, economic development and industrialization supported the emergence of a mass consumer society. Large numbers of Japanese who had previously resided in villages became urbanized; Tokyo, whose population stood at about three million in 1945, reached some nine million by 1970. Initial close ties to the United States fostered by the Mutual Security Treaty gave way to occasional tensions over American policies toward Vietnam, China, and exchange rates. The first trade frictions, over Japanese textile exports, took place at that time. Meanwhile, foreign culture, as was the case in the 1920s, greatly influenced young urban dwellers, who in the postwar period broke with their own traditions and turned increasingly to Hollywood and American popular culture for alternatives. Japan's new international image was projected and enhanced by events such as the highly successful 1964 Olympic Summer Games and the Ōsaka World Exposition of 1970.

CHAPTER TWO

CHINA, HONG KONG, MACAU, AND TAIWAN

● ●

C hina's relative isolation from the outside world made possible over the centuries the flowering and refinement of the Chinese culture, but it also left China ill prepared to cope with that world when, from the mid-19th century, it was confronted by technologically superior foreign nations. There followed a century of decline and decrepitude, as China found itself relatively helpless in the face of a foreign onslaught. The trauma of this external challenge became the catalyst for a revolution that began in the early 20th century against the old regime and culminated in the establishment of a communist government in 1949.

The ports of Hong Kong and Macau in southern China were both under European colonization for many years. Beginning in 1898, Hong Kong was leased to the British for 99 years; since 1997 it has been a special administrative region of China. From 1513, Portuguese traders had a foothold in Macau, though China did not recognize Portuguese sovereignty over the territory. Portugal and China agreed that Macau would be returned to Chinese rule in 1997, also as a special administrative region.

China has also had a complicated relationship with Taiwan, which was ceded to the Japanese in 1895. After World War II, Taiwan became the refuge of the Nationalists, who had lost the Chinese Civil War to the communists. For several decades the international community recognized Taiwan's government as the rightful government of China, but by 1970, the People's Republic of China in Beijing was widely recognized by the UN and other countries. The government of the ROC continued to claim jurisdiction over the Chinese mainland, whereas the government of the People's Republic of China on the mainland claimed jurisdiction over Taiwan; both governments remained in agreement that the island is a *sheng* (province) of China.

CHINA FACES A WESTERN CHALLENGE, 1839–60

The opium question, the direct cause of the first Sino-British clash in the 19th century, began in the late 18th century as the British attempted to counter-balance their unfavourable China trade with traffic in Indian opium. After monopolizing the opium trade in 1779, the East India Company's government began to sell the drug at auction to private British traders in India, who shipped it to buyers in China. The silver acquired from the sale of opium in China was sold at Guangzhou for the company's bills of exchange, payable in London, and was used by the company to purchase its large annual tea cargo for sale in Europe. This "triangular trade" became a major vehicle for realizing the potential gains from the British conquest of India, providing a means to repatriate the company's Indian revenue in opium in the form of Chinese teas.

In 1819 the company began to handle larger amounts of opium. Substantial social and economic disruption followed in China, not only from the effects of the opium habit itself as it spread among the populace but from the corruption it engendered among petty officials and from a fall in the value of copper in China's bimetallic monetary system as silver was drained from the economy. The Beijing court repeatedly banned the opium imports but without success, because the prohibition itself promoted corruption among the officials and soldiers

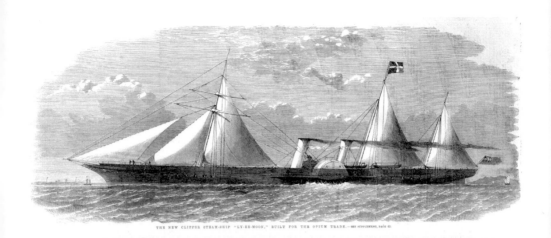

THE NEW CLIPPER STEAM-SHIP "LY-EE-MOON," BUILT FOR THE OPIUM TRADE.— SEE SUPPLEMENT, PAGE 42.

The clipper ship *Le-Rye-Moon* was one of many built for the opium trade.

concerned. There was no possibility of the opium question being solved as a domestic affair.

After the turn of the 19th century, the main avenue for opium smuggling was through the designated traders who were allowed only to manage the inter-Asian trade under the company's license. Without protection from the company, they cultivated the opium market in China on their own. They defied the opium ban in China and gradually became defiant toward Chinese law and order in general, having nothing in mind but making money. After Parliament revoked the East India Company's monopoly in 1834, William John Napier was appointed chief superintendent of British trade in China and arrived

at Guangzhou. He tried to negotiate with the Guangzhou authorities on equal footing, but the latter took
his behaviour as contrary to the established Sino-
foreign intercourse. His mission failed, and he was
replaced in 1836 by Charles (later Sir Charles) Elliot.

In Beijing a proposal in 1836 to relax the opium
restraint acquired much support, but the Daoguang
emperor appointed a radical patriot, Lin Zexu, as
imperial commissioner for an anti-opium campaign.
Chinese anti-opium efforts in fact began to make
considerable headway in controlling the Chinese side
of the smuggling trade in late 1838 and early 1839.
The critical foreign side of the opium trade was,
however, beyond Commissioner Lin's direct reach.
Arriving at Guangzhou in March 1839, Lin con-
fiscated and destroyed more than 20,000 chests of
opium. Skirmishes began after September between
the Chinese and the British.

THE FIRST OPIUM WAR AND ITS AFTERMATH

In February 1840 the British government decided
to launch a military expedition, and Elliot and his
cousin, George (later Sir George) Elliot, were appointed joint plenipotentiaries to China (though
the latter, in poor health, resigned in November).

In June, 16 British warships arrived in Hong Kong and sailed northward to the mouth of the Bei River to press China with their demands. Charles Elliot entered into negotiations with the Chinese, and, although an agreement was reached in January 1841, it was not acceptable to either government. In May 1841 the British attacked the walled city of Guangzhou (Canton) and received a ransom of $6 million, which provoked a counterattack on the part of the Cantonese. This was the beginning of a continuing conflict between the British and the Cantonese.

The Qing had no effective tactics against the powerful British navy. They retaliated merely by setting burning rafts on the enemy's fleet and encouraging people to take the heads of the enemies, for which they offered a prize. The imperial banner troops, although they sometimes fought fiercely, were ill-equipped and lacked training for warfare against the more-modern British forces. The Green Standard battalions were similarly in decay and without much motivation or good leadership. To make up the weakness, local militias were urgently recruited, but they were useless. The British proclaimed that their aim was to fight the government officials and soldiers who abused the people, not to make war against the Chinese population. And indeed there was a deep rift between the government and the people that the British could easily exploit, a weakness in Qing society that became apparent during the crisis of the war.

Elliot's successor, Henry Pottinger, arrived at Macau in August and campaigned northward, seizing Xiamen (Amoy), Dinghai, and Ningbo. Reinforced from India, he resumed action in May 1842 and took Wusong, Shanghai, and Zhenjiang. Nanjing yielded in August, and peace was restored with the Treaty of Nanjing. According to the main provisions of the treaty, China ceded Hong Kong to Britain, opened five ports to British trade, abolished the cohong system of trade, agreed to equal official recognition, and paid an indemnity of $21 million. This was the result of the first clash between China, which had regarded foreign trade as a favour given by the heavenly empire to the poor barbarians, and the British, to whom trade and commerce had become "the true herald of civilization."

The Treaty of Nanjing was followed by two supplementary arrangements with the British in 1843. In addition, in July 1844 China signed the Treaty of Wanghia (Wangxia) with the United States and in October the Treaty of Whampoa (Huangpu) with France. These arrangements made up a complex of foreign privileges by virtue of the most-favoured-nation clauses (guaranteeing trading equality) conceded to every signatory. All in all, they provided a basis for later inroads such as the loss of tariff autonomy, extraterritoriality (exemption from the application or jurisdiction of local law or tribunals), and the free movement of missionaries.

With the signing of the treaties—which began the so-called treaty-port system—the imperial commissioner Qiying, newly stationed at Guangzhou, was put in charge of foreign affairs. Following a policy of appeasement, his dealings with foreigners started fairly smoothly. But, contrary to the British expectation, the amount of trade dropped after 1846, and, to British dissatisfaction, the question of opium remained unsettled in the postwar arrangements. The core of the Sino-Western tension, however, rested in an antiforeign movement in Guangdong.

THE SECOND OPIUM WAR (ARROW WAR)

At the signing of the Treaty of Nanjing, China and Britain disagreed as to whether foreigners were allowed to enter the walled city of Guangzhou. Though Guangzhou was declared open in July 1843, the British faced Cantonese opposition. After 1847 trouble rapidly grew, and, as a result of an incident at nearby Foshan, a promise was given the British that they would be allowed to enter the city in 1849. Yet troubles continued. As a result of his inability to control the situation, Qiying was recalled in 1848 and replaced with the less-compliant Xu Guangjin. As the promised date neared, the Cantonese demonstrated against British entry. Finally, the British yielded, and the antiforeigners won a victory despite the fact that the Beijing court conceded a "temporary entrance" into the city.

After the Cantonese resistance in 1841, the gentry in Guangdong began to build a more-organized antiforeign movement, promoting the militarization of village society. The city of Guangzhou was also a centre of diffusion of xenophobia, because the scholars at the city's great academies were proclaiming the Confucian theory that uncultured barbarians should be excluded. The inspired antiforeign mood also contained a strong antigovernment sentiment and perhaps a tendency toward provincialism; the Cantonese rose up against the barbarians to protect their own homeland, without recourse to the government authorities.

In the strained atmosphere in Guangzhou, where the xenophobic governor-general, Ye Mingchen, was inciting the Cantonese to annihilate the British, the *Arrow* incident occurred in October 1856. Guangzhou police seized the *Arrow*, a Chinese-owned but British-registered ship flying a British flag, and charged its Chinese crew with piracy and smuggling. The British consul Harry Parkes sent a fleet to fight its way up to Guangzhou. French forces joined the venture on the plea that a French missionary had been officially executed in Guangxi. The British government sent an expedition under Lord Elgin as plenipotentiary. The Russians and the Americans abstained but sent their representatives for diplomatic maneuvering. At the end of 1857 an Anglo-French force occupied Guangzhou; in March 1858 they took the Dagu fort and marched to Tianjin.

The Qing representatives had no choice but to comply with the demands of the British and French; the Russian and U.S. diplomats also gained the privileges their militant colleagues secured by force. During June four Tianjin treaties were concluded that provided for, among other measures, the residence of foreign diplomats in Beijing and the freedom of Christian missionaries to evangelize their faith.

In 1859, when the signatories arrived off the Dagu fort on their way to sign the treaties in Beijing, they were repulsed, with heavy damage inflicted by the gunfire from the fort. In 1860 an allied force invaded Beijing, driving the Xianfeng emperor (reigned 1850–61) out of the capital to the summer palace at Chengde. A younger brother of the emperor, Gong

Qinwang (Prince Gong), was appointed imperial commissioner in charge of negotiation. The famous summer palace was destroyed by the British in October. Following the advice of the Russian negotiator, Prince Gong exchanged ratification of the 1858 treaties; in addition, he signed new conventions with the British and the French. The U.S. and Russian negotiators had already exchanged the ratification in 1859, but the latter's diplomatic performance in 1860 was remarkable.

Russian interests in the East had been activated in competition with the British effort to open China. A Russian spearhead, directed to Kuldja (Yining) by way of the Irtysh River, resulted in the Sino-Russian Treaty of Kuldja in 1851, which opened Kuldja and Chuguchak (Tacheng) to Russian trade. Another drive was directed to the Amur watershed under the initiative of Nikolay Muravyov, who had been appointed governor-general of eastern Siberia in 1847. By 1857 Muravyov had sponsored four expeditions down the Amur; during the third one, in 1856, the left bank and lower reaches of the river had actually been occupied by the Russians. In May 1858 Muravyov pressed the Qing general Yishan to sign a treaty at Aigun (Aihui), by which the territory on the northern bank of the Amur was ceded to Russia and the land between the Ussuri River and the sea was placed in joint possession by the two countries, pending further disposition. But Beijing refused to ratify the treaty. When the Anglo-French allies attacked northern China in 1860, the Russian negotiator Nikolay Ignatyev acted as China's friend and mediator in securing the evacuation of the invaders from Beijing. Soon after the allies had left Beijing, Ignatyev secured, as a reward for his mediatory effort, the Sino-Russian Treaty of Beijing, which confirmed the Treaty of Aigun and ceded to Russia the territory between the Ussuri and the sea.

The 1858–60 treaties extended the foreign privileges granted after the first Opium War and confirmed or legalized the developments in the treaty-port system. The worst effects for the Qing authorities were not the utilitarian rights, such as trade, commerce, and tariff, but the privileges that affected the moral and cultural values of China. The right to propagate Christianity threatened Confucian values, the backbone of the imperial system. The permanent residence of foreign representatives in Beijing signified an end to the long-established tributary relationship between China and other nations. The partial collapse of the tribute system meant a loss of the emperor's virtue, a serious blow to dynastic rule in China.

During the turbulent years 1858–60, the Qing bureaucracy was divided between the war and peace parties. It was the peace party's leaders—Prince Gong, Gui Liang, and Wen Xiang—who took charge of negotiating with the foreigners, though they did so not as a matter of principle but because the imminent crisis forced them to.

In 1861, in response to the settlement of the foreign representatives in the capital, the Zongli Yamen (office for General Management) was opened to deal with foreign affairs, its main staff filled by the peace party leaders. The Qing officials themselves, however, deemed this as still keeping a faint silhouette of the tribute system.

The delay and difficulty in the Qing adjustment to the Western presence may possibly be ascribed to both external and internal factors. The Chinese must have seen the Westerners who had appeared in China as purveyors of poisonous drugs and as barbarians in the full sense of the word, from whom they could learn nothing. But the Chinese staunchly held to their tradition, which also had two aspects—ideological and institutional. The core of the ideological aspect was the Confucian distinction between China and foreign nations. The institutional aspect had recently been much studied, however, and precedents in Chinese history had been found, for example, of treaty ports with foreign settlements, consular jurisdiction, and employment of Westerners as imperial personnel;

thus, the Chinese regarded the Western impact as an extension of their tradition rather than a totally new situation that necessitated a new adjustment. And at least until 1860 the Qing leaders remained withdrawn in the shell of tradition, making no effort to cope with the new environment by breaking the yoke of the past.

THE BOXER REBELLION

The crisis of 1896–98 stirred a furious antiforeign uprising in Shandong, aroused by the German advances and encouraged by the provincial governor. It was staged by a band of people called the Yihequan ("Righteous and Harmonious Fists"), who believed that a mysterious boxing art rendered them invulnerable to harm. The group's origin is generally supposed to have been in the White Lotus sect, though it may have begun as a self-defense organization during the Taiping Rebellion. At first the Boxers (as they were called in the West) directed their wrath against Christian converts, whom they vilified for having abandoned traditional Chinese customs in favour of an alien religion. Bands of Boxers roamed the countryside killing Chinese Christians and foreign missionaries. Developing from this anti-Christian hysteria, the Boxer Rebellion grew into a naive but furious attempt to destroy all things for-eign—including churches, railways, and mines—which the people blamed for their misery and for the loss of a sacred way of life.

Some Boxer recruits were disbanded imperial soldiers and local militiamen; others were Grand Canal boatmen deprived of a livelihood by the Western-built railways. Most recruits, though, came from the peasantry, which had suffered terribly from recent natural calamities in northern China. After 1895 the Huang He flooded almost annually, and in 1899–1900 a serious drought struck the north. Vast numbers of starving people turned to begging and banditry and were easy converts to the Boxers' cause.

Many local authorities refused to stop the vio-lence. Some supported the Boxers by incorporating them into local militias. The Manchu court, mean-while, was alarmed by the uncontrollable popular uprising but took great satisfaction at seeing revenge taken for its humiliation by the foreign powers. As a result, it assumed at first a neutral policy. On the part of the Boxers, there emerged sometime in the autumn of 1899 a move to gain access to the court under the slogan "Support for the Qing and exter-mination of foreigners." By May 1900 the Qing government had changed its policy and was secretly supporting the Boxers. Cixi inclined toward open war when she became convinced of the dependability of the Boxers' art. Finally, incensed over a false report that the foreign powers had demanded that she return administration to the emperor, she called on all Chinese to attack foreigners. Within days, on June 20, the Boxers' eight-week siege of the foreign legations in Beijing began; a day later Cixi declared war by ordering provincial governors to take part in the hostilities.

An international reinforcement of some 2,000 men had left Tianjin for Beijing before the siege, but on the way it was resisted by the Boxers and forced back to Tianjin. The foreign powers then sent an expedition of some 19,000 troops, which marched to Beijing and seized the city on August 14. Cixi and the emperor fled to Xi'an.

The two governors-general in the southeastern provinces, Liu Kunyi and Zhang Zhidong, who together with Li Hongzhang at Guangzhou had already disobeyed Beijing's antiforeign decrees, concluded an informal pact with foreign consuls at Shanghai on June 26, to the effect that the governors-general would take charge of the safety of the foreigners under their jurisdiction. At first the pact covered the five provinces in the Yangtze River region, but later it was extended to three coastal provinces. Thus, the foreign operations were restricted to Zhili (present-day Hebei) province, along the northern coast.

The United States, which had announced its commercial Open Door policy in 1899, made a second declaration of the policy in July 1900—this time insisting on the preservation of the territorial and administrative entity of China. With its newly acquired territory in the western Pacific, the United States was determined to preserve its own commercial interests in China by protecting Chinese territorial integrity from the other major powers. This provided a basis for the Anglo-German agreement (October 1900) for preventing further territorial partition, to which Japan and Russia consented. Thus, partition of China was avoided by mutual restraint among the powers.

The final settlement of the disturbance was signed in September 1901. The indemnity amounted to 450 million taels to be paid over 39 years. Moreover, the settlement demanded the establishment of permanent guards and the dismantling of forts between Beijing and the sea, a humiliation that made an independent China a mere fiction. In addition, the southern provinces were actually independent

THE OPEN DOOR POLICY

The Open Door policy was a statement of principles initiated by the United States in 1899 and 1900 for the protection of equal privileges among countries trading with China and in support of Chinese territorial and administrative integrity. The statement was issued in the form of circular notes dispatched by U.S. Secretary of State John Hay to Great Britain, Germany, France, Italy, Japan, and Russia. The Open Door policy was received with almost universal approval in the United States, and for more than 40 years it was a cornerstone of American foreign policy in East Asia.

The principle that all countries should have equal access to any of the ports open to trade in China had been stipulated in the Anglo-Chinese treaties of Nanjing (Nanking, 1842) and Wangxia (Wanghia, 1844). Great Britain had greater interests in China than any other power and successfully maintained the policy of the open door until the late 19th century. After the first Sino-Japanese War (1894–95), however, a scramble for "spheres of influence" in various parts of coastal China—

primarily by Russia, France, Germany, and Great Britain—began. Within each of those spheres the controlling major power claimed exclusive privileges of investment, and it was feared that each would likewise seek to monopolize the trade. Moreover, it was generally feared that the breakup of China into economic segments dominated by various great powers would lead to complete subjection and the division of the country into colonies.

The crisis in China coincided with several major developments in the United States. A new interest in foreign markets had emerged there following the economic depression of the 1890s. The United States also had just gained the Philippines, Guam, and Hawaii as a result of the Spanish-American War (1898) and was becoming increasingly interested in China, where American textile manufacturers had found markets for cheap cotton goods.

The 1899 Open Door notes provided that (1) each great power should maintain free access to a treaty port or to any other vested interest within its sphere, (2) only the Chinese government should collect taxes on trade, and (3) no great power having a sphere should be granted exemptions from paying harbour dues or railroad

(CONTINUED ON THE NEXT PAGE)

(CONTINUED FROM THE PREVIOUS PAGE)

charges. The replies from the various countries were evasive, but Hay interpreted them as acceptances.

In reaction to the presence of European armies in northern China to suppress the Boxer Rebellion (1900), Hay's second circular of 1900 stressed the importance of preserving China's territorial and administrative integrity. Hay did not ask for replies, but all the powers except Japan expressed agreement with those principles.

Japan violated the Open Door principle with its presentation of Twenty-one Demands to China in 1915. The Nine-Power Treaty after the Washington Conference (1921–22) reaffirmed the principle, however. The crisis in Manchuria (Northeast China) brought about by the Mukden Incident of 1931 and the war between China and Japan that broke out in 1937 led the United States to adopt a rigid stand in favour of the Open Door policy, including escalating embargoes on exports of essential commodities to Japan, notably oil and scrap metal. The embargoes are cited as one of the main reasons Japan went to war with the United States in late 1941. Japan's defeat in World War II (1945) and the communist victory in China's civil war (1949), which ended all special privileges to foreigners, made the Open Door policy meaningless.

during the crisis. These occurrences meant the collapse of the Qing prestige.

After the uprising, Cixi had to declare that she had been misled into war by the conservatives and that the court, neither antiforeign nor antireformist, would promote reforms, a seemingly incredible statement in view of the court's suppression of the 1898 reform movement. But the Qing court's antiforeign, conservative nationalism and the reforms undertaken after 1901 were in fact among several competing responses to the shared sense of crisis in early 20th-century China.

HONG KONG AS A BRITISH AND CHINESE COLONY

Before the British arrived in the mid-19th century, Hong Kong Island was inhabited only by a small fishing population, with few features to recommend it for settlement. It lacked fertile soil and fresh water, was mountainous, and was reputed to be a notorious haunt of pirates. But it was a relatively safe and undisturbed base for the British merchants who in 1821 began to use the fine harbour to anchor opium-carrying vessels. The great commercial and strategic significance of this deep, sheltered harbour, possessing east and west entrances and lying on the main trade routes of the Far East, was quickly realized.

After the first Opium War (1839–42), Hong Kong Island was ceded to Britain by the Treaty of Nanjing. The British were never satisfied with an incomplete control of the harbour, however. Less than 20 years later, after the second Opium War (1856–60), China was forced to cede the Kowloon Peninsula south of

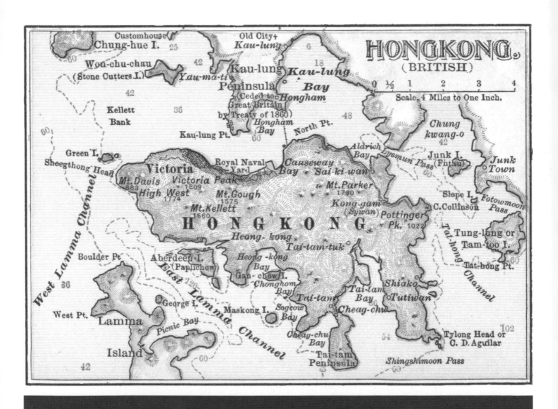

This map of Hong Kong dates from circa 1900, soon after the region was leased to Britain.

what is now Boundary Street and Stonecutters Island by the Convention of Beijing (1860). By the Convention of 1898, the New Territories together with 235 islands were leased to Britain for 99 years from July 1, 1898. With this expansion of territory, Hong Kong's population leaped to 120,000 in 1861 and to more than 300,000 by the end of the century.

Almost since its establishment, Hong Kong, more than any other treaty port, afforded a refuge for runaway persons and capital from China as well as an interim abode for rural emigrants destined for Southeast Asia and beyond. Such movements of Chinese people between China and Hong Kong were free and were highly responsive to the political and economic conditions in China. After the establishment of the Republic of China in 1912, proponents of emerging nationalism sought to abolish all foreign treaty privileges in China. A boycott against foreign goods particularly hurt Britain, which was well established in China. The campaign soon spread to Hong Kong, where strikes in the 1920s caused agitation.

When the Sino-Japanese War broke out in 1937, Hong Kong was once more a refuge, with thousands of Chinese fleeing to it before the advancing Japanese. With the outbreak of war in Europe in 1939, the position of the colony became more precarious, as it was now a target; the Japanese attacked and occupied Hong Kong in December 1941. During the war years Hong Kong's commerce was drastically impaired; food was scarce, and many residents fled to inland China. The population, which had numbered 1,600,000 in 1941, was reduced to about 650,000 by 1945 when the Japanese surrendered.

British troops returned to the city on Aug. 30, 1945, and civil government was reestablished in May 1946. Meanwhile, hundreds of thousands of Chinese and foreigners returned, and they were soon joined by economic and political refugees from China, who were fleeing the civil war between the Nationalist and communist armies.

The United Nations embargo in 1951 on trade with China and North Korea during the Korean War seriously curtailed the entrepôt trade, the lifeline of the colony, and for several years conditions were depressed. Hong Kong began its revival on the basis of light industries such as textiles, which were set up by immigrant capitalists and provided needed employment. These soon assumed their importance in the economy, providing as well the basis for further industrialization. But it was because much of the development depended on cheap labour, which toiled under extremely poor working conditions, that labour disputes and social discontent began to spread in the early 1960s. Severe riots broke out in

Hong Kong and Kowloon in May 1967 following a labour dispute in a plastic-flower factory. The economic and social unrest was immediately turned into violent political demonstrations, largely inspired by followers of the Cultural Revolution (1966–76) in China. When the situation stabilized toward the end of the 1960s, general working and living conditions were notably improved by labour legislation, large government housing projects, and extensive public works programs. Simultaneously, high-technology industries such as electronics were developed, and the property and financial markets prospered until early 1973, when the stock market collapsed as billions of dollars were drained out of Hong Kong. From the mid-1970s the economy resumed its upward trend as relations with China improved.

In the late 1970s, concern about the future of Hong Kong began to loom large, as British jurisdiction over the leased areas of the New Territories neared the 1997 expiration date. Although the lease applied only to the New Territories, the Chinese government had consistently maintained that the whole of Hong Kong was Chinese territory and considered that the question of the earlier Hong Kong–British agreements came under the category of unequal treaties and also required resolution. Initial contacts between the two governments on the matter were made from March 1979, but formal negotiations did not start until after the visit of the British prime minister to Beijing in September 1982. Negotiations continued for two years. Finally, the Chinese-British joint declaration on the question of Hong Kong was formally signed by the heads of the two governments in Beijing on Dec. 19, 1984. The agreement stipulated that Hong Kong (including Hong Kong Island, Kowloon, and the New Territories) would be recovered by China from July 1, 1997. There ensued a period of often difficult negotiations between Hong Kong and Beijing on the final wording of the document by which Hong Kong would be governed under Chinese sovereignty. Despite some reservations from Hong Kong, the National People's Congress formally ratified the Basic Law on April 4, 1990, which took effect on July 1, 1997, and established the Hong Kong Special Administrative Region directly under the Chinese central government.

The years after reunification generally were prosperous, as Hong Kong's economy experienced steady growth, despite its heavy dependence on global economic conditions. The already significant economic ties with the mainland increased even more dramatically than before reunification. In addition, major resources were devoted to improving the region's transportation infrastructure, which included new bridges and roadways in addition to the new airport. Politically, there were sustained calls for democratic reforms to the Basic Law that, at times, included large demonstrations and pressure from opposition-party members in the Legislative Council (LegCo). By the 2004 legislative elections, Beijing was allowing half of the LegCo seats to be directly elected from geographic constituencies, with the other half selected from business and professional groups known as "functional constituencies."

MACAU AS A PORTUGUESE AND CHINESE COLONY

The first Portuguese ship anchored in the Pearl River estuary in 1513, and further Portuguese visits followed regularly. Trade with China commenced in 1553. Four years later Portuguese paying tribute to China settled in Macau, which became the official and principal entrepôt for all international trade with China and Japan and an intermediary port for ships traveling from Lisbon to Nagasaki (at the time, Japan's only outport for trade); China, nonetheless, still refused to recognize Portuguese sovereignty over the territory. The first governor was appointed in the 17th century, but the Portuguese remained largely under the control of the Chinese. Missionaries carried over on Portuguese ships transformed Macau into an East Asian centre of Christianity. Even though China's trade with the outside world was gradually centralized in Guangzhou (Canton) toward the end of the 18th century, merchants were allowed into Guangzhou only during the trading season—from November to May—and the international merchant community established itself at Macau. By the mid-19th century the British colony of Hong Kong had surpassed Macau in trade, and within a few years the merchants had largely deserted the Portuguese possession, which never again was a major entrepôt.

In the 1930s and '40s Macau, declared a neutral territory during the Sino-Japanese War and World War II, became a refuge for both Chinese and Europeans. The Chinese population in the territory continued to grow when the communist government assumed power in China in 1949. In 1951 Portugal officially made Macau an overseas province. Following a military coup in Portugal in 1974, the government allotted more administrative autonomy and economic independence to the territory. The constitution promulgated in 1976 established the Legislative Assembly, which was dominated by the minority Portuguese. Until diplomatic relations were solidified between Portugal and the communist government in China in 1979, discussions on transferring Macau to Chinese control were fruitless.

In March 1984 the Portuguese governor dissolved the assembly in response to opposition within the government to extend the right to vote to the Chinese majority. A few months later new elections, which included Chinese suffrage, finally brought a significant number of Chinese deputies into the government. In April 1987 Portugal and China reached an agreement to return Macau to Chinese rule in 1999, using the Hong Kong Joint Declaration between Britain and China as a model. They agreed to provisions under the Basic Law that would ensure the autonomy of Macau for 50 years after the start of Chinese rule. These included Macau's right to elect local leaders, the right of its residents to travel freely, and the right to maintain its way of life, both economically and socially. Defense and foreign policy matters were to be administered by China, and those living in Macau without Portuguese passports would become Chinese citizens. Elections continued to turn out record numbers of voters and a Chinese majority legislature. On Dec. 20, 1999, Macau became a special administrative region under Chinese sovereignty, as Hong Kong had in 1997.

The period since reunification has been peaceful and marked by increasing prosperity. Much of the region's economic growth has come from the tremendous expansion in gambling and gaming since 2000, which transformed Macau into one of the world's largest gambling centres (in terms of revenue). Tourism also has risen sharply from levels in the 1990s. Major infrastructure projects have included continued land reclamation throughout the region and a third bridge (opened 2005) between Macau Peninsula and Taipa Island. The political situation has been stable, with orderly legislative elections. Ho Hau Wah (Edmund Ho) was named Macau's first chief executive at reunification in 1999; he was reelected to a second term in 2004.

TAIWAN UNDER THE JAPANESE AND CHINESE

Taiwan was known to the Chinese as early as the 3rd century AD, but settlement by the Chinese was not significant until the first quarter of the 17th century after recurrent famines in Fukien Province encouraged emigration of Fukienese from the mainland. Before then the island was a base of operations for Chinese and Japanese pirates. The Portuguese, who first visited the island in 1590 and named it Ilha Formosa ("Beautiful Island"), made several unsuccessful attempts at settlement. The Dutch and Spaniards established more lasting settlements, the Dutch at An-p'ing in southwestern Taiwan in 1624, the Spaniards in 1626 at Chi-lung in the north. Until 1646, when the Dutch seized the Spanish settlements, northern Taiwan was under Spanish domination, the south under Dutch control. The Dutch were expelled in 1661 by Cheng Ch'eng-kung, a man of mixed Chinese-Japanese parentage and a supporter of the defeated Ming emperors, who used the island as a centre of opposition to the Qing (Manchu) regime.

In 1683, 20 years after Cheng Ch'eng-kung's death, the island fell to the Qing and became part of Fukien Province. Meanwhile, sizable migrations of refugees, Ming supporters, had increased the population to about 200,000. As migrants streamed in from southeastern China, large areas in the north were settled. T'ai-nan (then called T'ai-wan) was the capital. By 1842 the population was estimated at 2,500,000, and both rice and sugar had become important exports to mainland China. In 1858 the Treaty of T'ien-ching (Tientsin) designated two Taiwan ports as treaty ports, T'ai-nan and Tan-shui, the latter a river port, long used as a port of call under the Spanish and Dutch, and downstream from the growing city of Taipei. Tea became an important export crop, and the island's trade centre shifted to the north, particularly to Tan-shui, where British trading companies established their headquarters.

Japan's continued interest in the island was reflected in a Japanese punitive expedition of 1874 ostensibly to protect the lives of Ryukyu fishermen along the island's coasts. The French blockaded the island during the undeclared Sino-French war of 1884–85 and occupied Chi-lung for a short period. In 1886 Taiwan became a separate province of China with a legal capital at T'ai-chung and a temporary capital at Taipei, which became the legal capital in 1894.

In 1895, as a result of the Treaty of Shimonoseki after the Sino-Japanese War, China ceded Taiwan and the Pescadores Islands to Japan, and the Japanese occupied Taipei in June of that year over the violent opposition of the Taiwanese population. For several months a Republic of Taiwan was in existence, but it was overcome by Japanese forces. The Japanese also faced the hostility of the aborigines, some of whom remained uncontrolled until the outbreak of the Pacific war. Taiwan was developed as a supplier of rice and sugar for Japan. Irrigation projects, agricultural extension services, and improvements in transportation and power supplies led to rapid increases in Taiwan's gross domestic product. Japanese policy was oriented toward the Japanization of the Taiwanese; Japanese was the language of instruction in a widespread basic educational system, and even after the end of World War II Japanese remained a lingua franca among the various Chinese dialect groups. In the 1930s Japanese economic policy shifted toward the development of industries based on relatively cheap hydroelectric power. Nevertheless, rice and sugar remained the basis of Taiwan's prewar export trade, almost all of which was directed toward Japan. Imports consisted largely of diverse manufactures from Japan. During World War II, Taiwan was a major staging area for Japan's invasion of Southeast Asia.

Taiwan was returned to China in 1945, after Japan was defeated in World War II. The Nationalist

As part of the "Japanization" of Taiwan, children were taught Japanese instead of Chinese in school.

government of China treated the island as conquered territory and regarded the people of Taiwan as collaborators with the Japanese enemy. Relations between the two steadily worsened, and the Taiwanese revolted in 1947. The Chinese put down the uprising, killing thousands of Taiwanese. The Chinese then faced the major problem, however, of winning back the trust and support of the Taiwanese, especially after the communist forces conquered the mainland in 1949. Large numbers of Nationalist government officials, troops, and other refugees from the mainland then fled to Taiwan. Chiang Kai-shek, who had been the leader of the Nationalist government of China, established his government on the island.

The United States at first withdrew support of the Nationalist government. However, after North Korea invaded South Korea in 1950, the United States changed its policy. In the Korean War, the People's Republic of China supported North Korea, while the United States aided South Korea. The United States thus began providing military support to the Republic of China. This support was formalized in a mutual security treaty signed in 1954.

After the People's Republic of China was admitted to the United Nations in 1971 and Taiwan was expelled, many countries began to switch their diplomatic ties from the Nationalists to the communists.

On Jan. 1, 1979, the United States ended diplomatic relations with Taiwan and granted diplomatic recognition to the People's Republic of China.

The governments of both Taiwan and mainland China agree that Taiwan is a province of China. Some groups in Taiwan have called for Taiwan to become an independent country, but the government of mainland China is firmly opposed to this. Taiwan has made great economic progress and is now one of the wealthiest and most industrialized parts of Asia.

CHAPTER THREE

KOREA

• •

The Chosŏn (Yi) dynasty, with 26 monarchs, ruled Korea from 1392 until the Japanese annexation in 1910. In 1592 Toyotomi Hideyoshi, the Japanese military leader who had just reunified Japan, sent a large force to Korea in an alleged attempt to invade China. The Korean land forces suffered a series of defeats, but Korean naval forces, led by Adm. Yi Sun-shin, secured full control of the sea. Yi won the greatest naval victories in Korean history, over the Japanese squadrons off Korea's southern coast. The national crisis brought people of almost all ranks, including Buddhist monks, to volunteer in fighting the Japanese. Ming China also dispatched troops to aid Korea. After one year the Japanese were forced to retreat, although another invasion followed in 1597. After Toyotomi's sudden death in 1598 the Japanese withdrew. The war left most of

Korea in ruins. Palaces, public buildings, and private homes were burned, and many cultural treasures were lost or destroyed. Scholars and artisans were kidnapped to Japan, where they were forced to teach Korea's advanced technology.

In the early 17th century nomadic Manchu violated the borders of both Ming China and Korea. Ming and Korean punitive attacks on Manchu strongholds in 1619 were beaten back, and in 1627 the Manchu overran northern Korea. Only after Korea had agreed to recognize their demand for "brotherhood" did the Manchu withdraw from the occupied territory. In 1636 the Manchu captured Seoul and wrested an unconditional surrender from the king. The Manchu then overthrew the Ming and in 1644 established the Qing dynasty; the tribute that Korea had paid to the Ming was switched to the Qing.

CONTACT WITH WORLD POWERS

King Kojong was too young to rule when he ascended the throne in 1864, and his father, Yi Ha-ŭng, known as the Taewŏn-gun ("Prince of the Great Court"), became the de facto ruler. The Taewŏn-gun set out to restore the powers of the monarchy and pursued a policy of national exclusionism. He put into force bold political reforms, such as faction-free recruitment of officials and the closing of many private Confucian academies.

During his rule, Western men-of-war and merchant vessels came in search of trade and friendship, but the Taewŏn-gun refused them. Korean soldiers and civilians burned and sank the American merchant ship *General Sherman* at P'yŏngyang in retaliation for lawless acts committed by the crew. Koreans repulsed two attacks by French warships in 1866. In 1871 an American flotilla came to obtain a shipwreck convention but, encountering Korean resistance, left. Such incidents strengthened the Taewŏn-gun's resolve to keep the country's doors closed.

Japan repeatedly made futile attempts to establish diplomatic relations with Korea. The Japanese militarists thereupon raised an outcry for a war of conquest on Korea. Meanwhile, the Taewŏn-gun came under widespread criticism for the enormous financial burden he had imposed on the people. He relinquished his power in 1873 in favour of Kojong. Queen Min and her relatives took over the helm of state and initiated policies opposed to those of the Taewŏn-gun. Japan, which had been watching developments in Korea, dispatched a squadron of warships and pressured Korea to sign a treaty of commerce and friendship. The ports of Pusan (Busan), Wŏnsan, and Inch'ŏn (Incheon) were subsequently opened to Japanese trade.

The growing Japanese presence in Korea was disturbing to the rulers of Qing China. When conservative Korean soldiers tried to restore the Taewŏn-gun, the Qing used it as a pretext for stationing troops in Korea. Thus began a period of aggressive Chinese interference in Korean affairs. China forced Korea to sign a trade agreement that heavily favoured Chinese merchants. Korea signed a treaty of commerce and friendship with the United States (1882) through the good offices of China. Similar treaties with the United Kingdom, Germany, Russia, and France followed, and foreign missions were established in Seoul.

Once the doors were opened, a modernization movement began. Students and officials were sent to Japan and China; Western-style schools and newspapers were founded. The government, however, could not proceed with a consistent policy of modernization, for the king was mentally incompetent and the ruling class was divided into radicals and moderates.

In 1884 the radicals seized power in a coup d'état and formulated a bold blueprint for reform. Chinese troops, however, moved in and overthrew their three-day-old regime. This led in 1885 to the signing of the Li-Itō Convention, designed to guarantee a Sino-Japanese balance of power on the Korean peninsula.

THE TONGHAK UPRISING AND GOVERNMENT REFORM

Government expenditures greatly increased, largely because of appropriations for machinery imports and government reorganization, and the difficult financial situation was aggravated by obligations to pay reparations to Japan. Heavier tax levies were imposed on peasants, who provided the bulk of government revenue. The import of such necessities as cotton textiles upset the traditional self-sufficiency of the farming community. Furthermore, usurious loans by Japanese rice dealers contributed to reducing the peasantry to abject poverty. Angry peasants turned increasingly to Ch'ŏndogyo (Tonghak).

Despite ruthless government persecution, Ch'ŏndogyo took deep root in the peasantry. Its followers staged large-scale demonstrations calling for an end to injustice. A negative official response precipitated the Tonghak Uprising (1894), in which the Ch'ŏndogyo followers and the peasantry formed a united front to demand reform. Government troops armed with Western weapons suffered ignominious defeats in the southern provinces, weakening the government's military grip on the country. Foreign intervention seemed the last resort open to the rulers, and

Chinese troops soon moved in at the request of the government. Simultaneously, Japan, without invitation, dispatched a large military contingent, and the two foreign powers were in sharp and sudden confrontation.

The rebels laid down their arms voluntarily to defuse the threat, but the Sino-Japanese War broke out in July 1894. Japan emerged victorious, and the two belligerents signed the Treaty of Shimonoseki in April 1895, which recognized Japanese hegemony in Korea.

Japanese troops celebrate their victory at Asan during the Sino-Japanese War.

At the instigation of the Japanese, the Korean government initiated a wide range of reforms during the war. It set up a Council of Deliberations to undertake reforms, issued pertinent decrees, and formed Western-style institutions and a cabinet. Civil service examinations were discontinued, and such social practices as class discrimination were abolished. Public reaction to the reforms was unfavourable. The government realized that old customs and institutions would die hard and that reform would take more than mere decrees and imitation of things Western.

THE INTERNATIONAL POWER STRUGGLE AND KOREA'S RESISTANCE

Japan's supremacy in Korea and its subsequent acquisition of the Liaodong Peninsula in Manchuria were more than Russia, with its long-cherished dream of southward expansion in East Asia, could tolerate. With German and French support, Russia pressured Japan to return the peninsula to China. At the same time, encouraged by Russia, the Korean government began to take an anti-Japanese course. The Japanese thereupon engineered the assassination of Queen Min (October 1895), the suspected mastermind behind the anti-Japanese stance. Fearing for his own life, King Kojong took refuge in the Russian legation, where he granted such concessions as mining and lumbering franchises to Russia and other powers.

A popular movement for the restoration of Korean sovereignty arose under the leadership of such figures as Sŏ Chae-p'il (Philip Jaisohn). Returning from many years of exile, Sŏ organized in 1896 a political organization called the Independence Club (Tongnip Hyŏphoe). He also published a daily newspaper named *Tongnip sinmun* ("The Independent") as a medium for awakening the populace to the importance of sovereignty and civil rights. On the urging of the Tongnip Hyŏphoe, the king returned to his palace and declared himself emperor and his kingdom the Great Korean (Tae Han) Empire.

The Boxer Rebellion in China (1900) led to a Russian invasion of Manchuria and to the Russo-Japanese War (1904–05). The Korean government at first declared neutrality, but under Japanese pressure it signed an agreement allowing Japan to use much of its territory for military operations against the Russians.

Japan was the victor, and the resulting Treaty of Portsmouth (September 1905), signed through the mediation of the United States, granted Japan undisputed supremacy in Korea. Its hand thus strengthened, Japan forced the Korean emperor into signing a treaty that made Korea a Japanese protectorate (November 1905).

Subsequently, the Korean emperor secretly dispatched an emissary to the international peace conference held at The Hague in 1907 to urge the great powers to intercede with Japan on behalf of Korea. The mission failed, however, and served only to infuriate Japan. Under Japanese coercion, Emperor Kojong then abdicated in favour of his son, Emperor Sunjong. The Korean army was disbanded, and in 1910 Japan annexed Korea.

A section of the Korean army led by deposed officials and Confucian scholars took up arms against the Japanese in the southern provinces following the 1905 treaty. For five years anti-Japanese guerrilla units, called the "righteous armies," effectively harassed the Japanese occupation forces, especially in 1908–09. With the annexation, however, they were driven into Manchuria. Large numbers of Koreans emigrated to Manchuria, Siberia, and Hawaii before and after 1910.

KOREA UNDER JAPANESE RULE

Japan set up a government in Korea in which the governor-generalship was filled by generals or admirals appointed by the Japanese emperor. The Koreans were deprived of freedom of assembly, association, the press, and speech. Many private schools were closed because they did not meet certain arbitrary standards. The colonial authorities used their own school system as a tool for assimilating Korea to Japan, placing primary emphasis on teaching the Japanese language and excluding from the educational curriculum such subjects as Korean language and Korean history. The Japanese built nationwide transportation and communications networks and established a new monetary and financial system. They also promoted Japanese commerce in Korea while barring Koreans from similar activities.

The colonial government promulgated a land-survey ordinance that forced landowners to report the size and area of their land. By failing to do this, many farmers were deprived of their land. Farmland and forests owned jointly by a village or a clan were likewise expropriated by the Japanese since no single individual could claim them. Much of the land thus expropriated was then sold cheaply to Japanese. Many of the dispossessed took to the woods and subsisted by slash-and-burn tillage, while others emigrated to Manchuria and Japan in search of jobs; the majority of Korean residents now in those areas are their descendants.

A turning point in Korea's resistance movement came on March 1, 1919, when nationwide anti-Japanese rallies were staged. The former emperor, Kojong, the supreme symbol of independence, had died a few weeks earlier, bringing mourners from all parts of the country to the capital for his funeral. A Korean Declaration of Independence was read at a rally in Seoul on March 1. Waves of students and citizens took to the streets, demanding independence. An estimated two million people took part. The March First Movement, as it came to be known, took the form of peaceful demonstrations, appealing to the conscience of the Japanese. The Japanese, however, responded with brutal repression, unleashing their gendarmerie and army and navy units to suppress the demonstrations. They arrested some 47,000 Koreans, of whom about 10,500 were indicted, while some 7,500 were killed and 16,000 wounded.

In September independence leaders, including Yi Tong-nyŏng and An Ch'ang-ho, who in April had formed a Korean provisional government in Shanghai, elected Syngman Rhee as president. It brought together all Korean exiles and established an efficient liaison with leaders inside Korea. Japan realized that its iron rule required more sophisticated methods. The gendarmerie gave way to an ordinary constabulary force, and partial freedom of the press was granted. But the oppressive and exploitative Japanese colonial policy remained ruthless, though using less conspicuous methods.

Taking advantage of a wartime business boom, Japan took leaps forward as a capitalist country. Korea became not only a market for Japanese goods but also a fertile region for capital investment. Meanwhile, industrial development in Japan was achieved at the sacrifice of agricultural production, creating a chronic shortage of rice. The colonial government undertook projects for increasing rice production throughout Korea. Many peasants were ordered to turn their dry fields into paddies. The program was temporarily suspended during the worldwide economic depression in the early 1930s. It soon resumed, however, in order to meet the increased needs of the Japanese military in its war against China, which began in 1931. Most Koreans were forced to subsist on low-quality cereals imported from Manchuria instead of their own rice.

Of the several dailies and magazines founded shortly after the March First Movement, the newspapers *Dong-A Ilbo* ("East Asia Daily") and *Chosun Ilbo* ("Korea Daily") spoke the loudest for the Korean people and inspired them with the ideals of patriotism and democracy. In the academic community, scholars conducted studies on Korean culture and tradition. Novels and poems in colloquial Korean enjoyed new popularity.

A major anti-Japanese mass rally was held in Seoul in 1926, on the occasion of the funeral of Emperor Sunjong. A nationwide student uprising originated in Kwangju in November 1929, demanding an end to Japanese discrimination. These and other resistance movements were led by a wide spectrum of Korean intellectuals.

In 1931 the Japanese imposed military rule once again. After the outbreak of the second Sino-Japanese War (1937) and of World War II in the Pacific (1941), Japan attempted to obliterate Korea as a nation: Koreans were forced to worship at Japanese Shintō shrines and even to adopt Japanese-style names, and academic societies devoted to Korean studies as well as newspapers and magazines published in Korean were banned. The Japanese desperately needed additional manpower to replenish the dwindling ranks of their military and labour forces. As a consequence,

COMFORT WOMEN

Comfort women (also called military comfort women, or, in Japanese, *jūgun ianfu*) was a euphemism for women who provided sexual services to Japanese Imperial Army troops during Japan's militaristic period that ended with World War II and who generally lived under conditions of sexual slavery. Estimates of the number of women involved typically range up to 200,000, but the actual number may have been even higher. The great majority of them were from Korea (then a Japanese protectorate), though women from China, Taiwan, and other parts of Asia—including Japan and Dutch nationals in Indonesia—were also involved.

From 1932 until the end of the war in 1945, comfort women were held in brothels called "comfort stations" that were established to enhance the morale of Japanese soldiers and ostensibly to reduce random sexual assaults. Although some of the women may have participated voluntarily, the great many of them were often lured by false promises of employment or were abducted

(CONTINUED ON THE NEXT PAGE)

(CONTINUED FROM THE PREVIOUS PAGE)

and sent against their will to comfort stations, which existed in all Japanese-occupied areas, including China and Burma (Myanmar). Comfort stations were also maintained within Japan and Korea. The women typically lived in harsh conditions, where they were subjected to continual rapes and were beaten or murdered if they resisted.

The Japanese government had an interest in keeping soldiers healthy and wanted sexual services under controlled conditions, and the women were regularly tested for sexually transmitted diseases and infections. According to several reports—notably a study sponsored by the United Nations that was published in 1996—many of the comfort women were executed at the end of World War II. The women who survived often suffered physical maladies (including sterility), psychological illnesses, and rejection from their families and communities. Many survivors in foreign countries were simply abandoned by the Japanese at the end of the war and lacked the income and means of communication to return to their homes.

In 1990 the South Korean government set up the Korean Council for the Women Drafted for Military Sexual Slavery by Japan after initial Japanese denial of responsibility. The council asked for an admittance of culpability, an apology, a memorial, and financial compensation for victims and that Japanese textbooks be appropriately altered to reflect the realities of the sexual slavery. The Japanese government denied evidence of coercing comfort women and rejected calls for compensation, saying that the 1965 treaty between Japan and South Korea had settled all outstanding matters.

The issue of comfort women gained international awareness in 1991, when a group of surviving women, breaking decades of silence,

Many comfort women who survived the war struggled to recover, both physically and mentally.

(CONTINUED ON THE NEXT PAGE)

(CONTINUED FROM THE PREVIOUS PAGE)

filed a class-action lawsuit against the Japanese government. The women and their supporters sued for compensation on the grounds of human rights violations. At about the same time, Yoshimi Yoshiaki, a historian from Chuo University in Tokyo, discovered documents in the archives of Japan's Self-Defense Force and published a report of his findings that linked the Japanese wartime military and government to the maintenance of the comfort-women system.

In 1991 the Japanese government admitted publicly for the first time that comfort stations had existed during the war. Two years later, in a statement issued by the chief cabinet minister, the government also acknowledged its involvement in the recruitment of comfort women and its deception of those women, and it apologized for affronting their honour. Although the Japanese government denied any legal responsibility for the sexual assaults, it set up the Asian Women's Fund in 1995 as an attempt at resolution. However, the fund was sustained from donations from private citizens, not government monies, and Korean activists opposed its existence. The fund ceased operating in 2007.

hundreds of thousands of able-bodied Koreans, both men and women, were drafted to fight for Japan and to work in mines, factories, and military bases. In addition, after the start of the Pacific war, the Japanese forced thousands of Korean women to provide sexual services (as "comfort women") for the military.

When Shanghai fell to the Japanese, the Korean provisional government moved to Chongqing in southwestern China. It declared war against Japan in December 1941 and organized the Korean Restoration Army, composed of independence fighters in China. This army fought with the Allied forces in China until the Japanese surrender in August 1945, which ended 35 years of Japanese rule over Korea.

In the late 20th century, the Japanese government sought to address lingering animosities that existed toward Japan on the Korean peninsula. Formal statements of apology to Korea for Japan's colonial rule were issued (most notably by Prime Minister Murayama Tomiichi in 1995), visits were made by the leaders of Japan and South Korea to each other's countries, and bilateral trade agreements were negotiated. However, such positive steps tended to be offset by events that often angered South Korea: occasional statements by Japanese government officials that seemed to defend Japan's colonial and wartime actions (including the forced prostitution of

Korean women during the war), continued periodic prime ministerial visits to the Yasukuni Shrine, and revelations that Japan's colonial rule was positively depicted in Japanese textbooks. A further issue for South Korea was the status of Koreans living in Japan, many of whom were third- or fourth-generation Japanese-born. Despite these differences, in 2002 Japan and South Korea cohosted the association football (soccer) World Cup finals, the first time the event was held in Asia or staged jointly by two countries.

CHAPTER FOUR

MONGOLIA

• •

From 1691 northern Mongolia was colonized by Qing (Manchu) China. With the collapse of Qing rule in Mongolia in 1911/12, the Bogd Gegeen (or Javzandamba), Mongolia's religious leader, was proclaimed Bogd Khan, or head of state. He declared Mongolia's independence, but only autonomy under China's domain was achieved. From 1919, nationalist revolutionaries, with Soviet assistance, drove out Chinese troops attempting to reoccupy Mongolia, and in 1921 they expelled the invading White Russian cavalry. July 11, 1921, then became celebrated as the anniversary of the revolution. The Mongolian People's Republic was proclaimed in November 1924, and the Mongolian capital, centred on the main monastery of the Bogd Gegeen, was renamed Ulaanbaatar ("Red Hero").

THE ASCENDANCY OF THE MANCHU

The rise of the Qing (Manchu) dynasty, which had such profound effects on the fate of Mongolia, began long before 1644, the year a Manchu emperor was first seated on the throne in Beijing. In the late 16th century it was becoming clear that a new barbarian conquest of China was again possible. In competition with the various Mongol princes and tribes already mentioned, the Manchu had the advantage that in the southern part of northeastern China (Manchuria), but outside the Great Wall, there was a large Chinese population with a number of urban centres and a flourishing trade that, instead of passing by land through the Great Wall, went largely by sea to the Shandong Peninsula—to the rear, that is, of the rulers in Beijing. These Chinese were somewhat alienated from other Chinese. They had for centuries been accustomed to trading with the barbarians and to farming under the patronage of barbarian princes, and they did not like Beijing's periodic attempts to maintain a "closed frontier" along the Great Wall.

The Manchu not only subjugated these Chinese but also cultivated their loyalty and were soon heavily dependent on them, not only economically but for military manpower. To balance this dependence, they

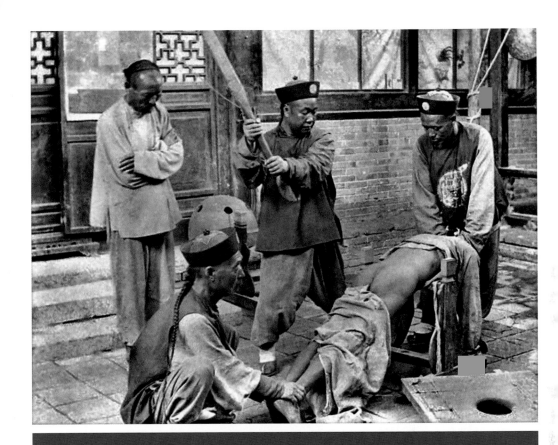

Punishment in Manchu China was often harsh.

built up a network of alliances with their other neighbours, the easternmost Mongols, and Mongol troops took part in the Manchu conquest of China. Before the Manchu occupied Beijing, they established control of the southern fringe of Mongolia, which they organized as part of their military reserve for the domination of China. This organization is the origin of the institutional and administrative concept of "Inner" Mongolia. It took the Manchu about a century to add northern, or "Outer," Mongolia to their empire, resulting in two Mongolias markedly different from each other, Inner Mongolia being much more closely integrated with China.

Meanwhile, the Oirat (Jungar) made a belated effort to unite all the Mongols in rivalry with the Manchu. The Oirat were strengthened by their control of a number of the East Turkistan oases but weakened by rivalries among their chiefs, by the diversion of much of their strength to adventures in Tibet, and by the reluctance of the Khalkh princes to accept the overlordship of princes not descended from Genghis Khan. Led by such warriors as Galdan (Dga'-ldan), the Oirat made sweeping campaigns far to the east in Mongolia but were never quite able to consolidate their gains.

Unwilling to accept submission to the Oirat as the price of unification, the Khalkh princes rallied more and more to the Manchu, who guaranteed their aristocratic privileges and titles in a great convention at Dolon Nor (Duolun), Inner Mongolia, in 1691. With the added resources of Khalkh, the Manchu were then able to mount a long series of military campaigns in which they annihilated the Oirat power with tremendous slaughter.

This conquest was not completed until 1759, however, and it was complicated by many events, particularly a major revolt against Manchu rule in western Khalkh in the 1750s led by a noble named Chingünjav. He was a coconspirator with an Oirat leader named Amursanaa, who in turn had first submitted to the Manchu and then rebelled against them. This was the last period of general warfare involving the Mongols, and it ended with a considerable redistribution of the tribes; several Khalkh groups that had fled from the Oirat into Inner Mongolia never returned; a few Chahar from Inner Mongolia were settled in East Turkistan as garrisons; numbers of the Oirat group were included in the western part of Khalkha geographically but not within the tribal organization; some ended their migrations at the Alxa Plateau (Ala Shan Desert), at the western end of Inner Mongolia, but not within the Inner Mongolian organization; and some ended theirs far away in the Koko Nor–Qaidam Basin region of Tibet.

The most distant Oirat wanderers (mostly Torguud and Dörvöd) had migrated in the early 17th century from the Altai Mountains to the Volga River, where they took service under the tsars and participated in the Russian conquest of the Caucasus region. In 1771 about 70,000 families migrated all the way back to East Turkistan—which by then had been renamed Xinjiang ("New Frontier") by the Manchu—where they were accepted under Manchu rule and allotted pastures for grazing. The descendants of those who remained on the Volga were known as the Kalmyk (Kalmuck).

The ensuing period of peace degenerated into stagnation and economic decline. Chinese camp followers had accompanied the Manchu conquest, and from this grew Chinese control of the caravan trade and of a barter trade exploiting usurious terms of credit. Because Mongol troops were of decreasing use for the control of China, there was no incentive for the Manchu to protect, economically, this source of manpower, and the Manchu authorities relied increasingly on the potentates of Tibetan Buddhism, who were themselves increasingly corrupt, for the control of Mongolia. Chinese colonization began to encroach on the pasturelands of Inner Mongolia, and at the end of the 19th century an attempt was made to plant a screen of Chinese colonists along the frontier between Siberia and Outer Mongolia.

INDEPENDENCE AND REVOLUTION

At the turn of the 20th century, Japan and Russia were competing to expand their empires into northeastern

Asia at the expense of the Qing (Manchu) rulers in China. Russia had encroached southward into northern Manchuria. Meanwhile, Japan had fought and won the Sino-Japanese War of 1894–95 and had demanded that China cede the Liaodong Peninsula and its strategically important harbours of Dalian (Dairen) and Port Arthur (Lüshun; now part of Dalian) on the Chinese coast. However, the Western powers intervened, and in 1898 Russia negotiated a 25-year lease of the peninsula with China, much to the anger of Japan. In the ensuing Russo-Japanese War (1904–05), Japan prevailed, and Russia ceded to Japan all its interests in northeastern China. In addition, by secret treaties concluded after the war, Inner Mongolia east of the meridian of Beijing was recognized by Russia as a Japanese sphere of interest.

Meanwhile, the British, concerned about a possible Russian threat to India through Tibet, which the Manchu could not control, sent an expeditionary force under Francis Younghusband to Lhasa. In 1904 the Dalai Lama fled Lhasa and took refuge in Urga (now Ulaanbaatar) with the Javzandamba *khutagt* (Mongolia's spiritual leader) for nearly two years. The agreement signed between Britain and Tibet in 1904 presented Tibet as an independent state and made no reference to Qing rule, although the Manchu *amban* (governor) was present at the signing.

However, in 1907 the Qing negotiated their own treaty with the British that recognized Chinese suzerainty in Tibet. In 1910 Chinese troops entered Lhasa, and the Dalai Lama again fled, though this time to India, returning in 1912. In a treaty signed at Niislel Khüree (now Ulaanbaatar) in January 1913, Tibet and Mongolia declared themselves both to be free from Manchu rule and separate from China, and they pledged to cooperate as sovereign states.

Mongolia at the start of the 20th century was agrarian, and its people were highly stratified socially and economically. There were two classes of vassals: the *khamjlaga*, who under Manchu law were serfs for life of the local nobility and civil administrators; and the *shavi*, the vassals of the monastery estates. Trade in essentials like tea, rice, and tobacco was in the hands of Chinese companies, which willingly extended credit at high interest rates. The currency consisted of units of livestock, as well as tea bricks, small silver ingots, and some foreign coins. When the officials and nobility got into debt, they would increase their taxes in kind on the population. As a result, many Mongols were impoverished and occasionally rebellious, despite the risk of terrible punishment at the hands of the Qing authorities, who had built fortified administrative centres and garrison towns like Khovd and Uliastai to control Mongolia's regions.

The Dalai Lama fled Lhasa when the British invaded Tibet in 1904.

By 1911, when the Chinese Revolution broke out, unrest was widespread in Mongolia. In December the Manchu *amban* was ordered to leave, the Javzandamba was proclaimed the Bogd Khan ("Holy King"), and he declared the independence of Mongolia—Inner Mongolia and Tannu Tuva (Tyva), as well as Outer Mongolia. Also at that time, the Bogd Khan's capital, Ikh Khüree ("Great Monastery"), was renamed Niislel Khüree ("Capital Monastery"). The Qing emperor abdicated in 1912, and the Republic of China was proclaimed.

Also that year Russia signed a treaty with the Bogd Khan's government that recognized Mongolia, although the interpretation of this recognition between the two parties differed: Mongolia considered itself independent of China, while Russia characterized Mongolia as being "autonomous." The Russian position was further underlined in 1913, when Russia and China issued a declaration stating that Mongolia was still under Chinese suzerainty. Mongolia objected, but this status was reinforced by a joint Russian-Chinese-Mongolian treaty in 1915, in which the Bogd Khan's government was obliged to accept autonomy under Chinese suzerainty. As a result, the Bogd Khan was unable to unite Inner with Outer Mongolia, nor was he able to prevent Russia from colonizing Tuva.

Soviet power was established in St. Petersburg following the Russian Revolution of 1917, and it gradually was extended eastward across Russia. In August 1919 the Soviet Russian government recognized Mongolian autonomy, but within a few months Chinese troops had occupied Niislel Khüree and deposed the Bogd Khan. During that turbulent period, Mongolian nationalists Dansrangiin Dogsom, Dogsomyn Bodoo, and others formed underground resistance groups and established contact with Russian Bolsheviks.

In June 1920 a group of these revolutionaries formed the Mongolian People's Party (MPP), and two months later several MPP members, including Soliin Danzan and Dambdyn Chagdarjav, were sent to Moscow to seek help from the Comintern (Third International) and to meet Bolshevik leader Vladimir Ilich Lenin. Two other revolutionaries, Damdiny Sükhbaatar and Khorloogiin Choibalsan, who had stayed in Siberia in the city of Irkutsk, made their way to the small town of Troitskosavsk on the border with Mongolia to organize the resistance. Meanwhile, tsarist cavalry units under the command of Baron Roman von Ungern-Sternberg (known as the "Mad Baron") entered Mongolia from eastern Siberia, advanced on Niislel Khüree, drove out the

Damdiny Sükhbaatar, cofounder and leader of the Mongolian People's Revolutionary Party, was the major force in the founding of the communist Mongolian People's Republic.

Chinese occupation forces, and in February 1921 restored the Bogd Khan to the throne under the baron's control.

The rule of the Mad Baron was cruel and bloody but relatively brief. In March 1921 the Mongolian revolutionaries gathered in Troitskosavsk and held the first MPP congress, where they adopted a program of action and appointed a provisional cabinet. A Mongolian revolutionary force was assembled under Sükhbaatar's command that, along with Soviet army units, advanced southward into Mongolia and in July 1921 captured Niislel Khüree. A "people's government" of Mongolia was appointed, with Bodoo as prime minister, and July 11 subsequently was celebrated as the anniversary of its establishment (now the first day of the *naadam* sports festival). The Bogd Khan was reinstated as a constitutional monarch with limited powers. The baron was captured in August, handed over to the Soviet authorities, and executed. In November Danzan and Sükhbaatar were sent to Moscow to meet Lenin, and the first Mongolian-Soviet treaty was concluded.

A power struggle ensued between nationalists and communists. In 1922 Bodoo and Chagdarjav were accused of "counterrevolutionary activities" and executed, and the situation was exacerbated by the death of Sükhbaatar in February 1923 and of the Bogd

Khan in May 1924. The third congress of the MPP was convened in August 1924, during which Danzan was accused of "bourgeois tendencies" and executed. At the congress, calls were made for Mongolia to develop a close friendship with the Soviet Union, to purge the country of "oppressor class elements," and to adopt a Leninist "noncapitalist path of development." In addition, either at the 1924 congress or early in 1925, the party was renamed the Mongolian People's Revolutionary Party (MPRP). A national assembly, the Great Khural, convened on November 8–26 and adopted Mongolia's first constitution, renaming the country the Mongolian People's Republic (MPR). The capital, Niislel Khüree, also was renamed Ulaanbaatar (Ulan Bator), meaning "Red Hero."

COUNTERREVOLUTION AND JAPAN

On the Bogd Khan's death, the limited monarchy lapsed, but the new MPR government obstructed the search for a reincarnation of the Javzandamba. By 1929 the government had instituted an official ban on recognizing any reincarnations. The 1920s were marked by violent swings in the MPRP's policies. In 1924–28 the party leadership pursued "Get rich!"

policies that later were described as "right opportunism," which were countered after a change in leadership by a period of "left deviation." The leftists soon began setting up herding communes on property expropriated from landlords and monasteries. These actions precipitated a series of insurrections that were finally suppressed by April 1932. Shortly thereafter, however, the Comintern decided that the Mongolian revolution had been progressing too rapidly and was not yet at the socialist stage of development, and the MPRP adopted more moderate policies—a trend that became known as the "new turn."

The MPRP congress held in October 1934 drew attention to a new threat to Mongolia: that from Japan. In 1927 Tanaka Giichi, then the Japanese prime minister, had called for a policy of Japanese expansion in East Asia. Japan already had established a strong presence in Manchuria, on Mongolia's eastern border, when on Sept. 18, 1931, the Japanese Kwantung Army staged the Mukden Incident as a pretext for occupying the city of Mukden (now Shenyang). Japanese troops soon occupied all of Manchuria, and in 1932 Japan established the puppet state of Manchukuo there. In 1933 Japan annexed Jehol province—situated on the border of Inner Mongolia and now divided between Hebei and Liaoning provinces—outright and claimed Outer Mongolia (i.e., the MPR) as part of Manchukuo. Mongolian and Kwantung Army troops clashed at Lake Buir on Mongolia's eastern border in 1935, prompting the Soviet and Mongolian governments to sign a mutual aid protocol in March 1936, in which they agreed to support one another in the event of attack. The Nationalist government in China protested this pact as being contrary to Chinese claims of suzerainty over Mongolia. In 1937 Japan annexed Chahar province (now in Inner Mongolia), on Mongolia's southeastern border, and then, following the Marco Polo Bridge Incident near Beijing (July 7), went to war with China.

The uncertainty, both internal and external, posed by the Japanese threat engendered political hysteria that developed into wholesale arrests and executions on charges of counterrevolutionary activity and spying for the Japanese. Khorloogiin Choibalsan, minister of internal affairs, with the help of the Soviet NKVD (secret police), had tens of thousands of innocent victims rounded up, who were forced to admit their "guilt" and then were executed. After Soviet leader Joseph Stalin pointed out that there were many more Buddhists than MPRP members in Mongolia, most of the country's monasteries and temples were destroyed, their treasures stolen, and their lamas shot or put to forced labour. Prominent Mongolians

THE MUKDEN INCIDENT

The Mukden Incident, also called the Manchurian Incident, refers to the seizure of the Manchurian city of Mukden (now Shenyang, Liaoning province, China) by Japanese troops in 1931. It was followed by the Japanese invasion of all of Manchuria (now Northeast China) and the establishment of the Japanese-dominated state of Manchukuo (Manzhouguo) in the area.

Throughout the early 20th century the Japanese had maintained special rights in Manchuria, and they had felt that the neutrality of the area was necessary for the defense of their colony in Korea. They were thus alarmed when their position in Manchuria was threatened by the increasingly successful unification of China in the late 1920s by the Chinese Nationalist leader Chiang Kai-shek (Jiang Jieshi), at the same time that Soviet pressures on Manchuria increased from the north. Responding to this pressure, officers of the Japanese Kwantung (Guandong) Army, which was stationed in Manchuria, initiated an incident

(CONTINUED ON THE NEXT PAGE)

(CONTINUED FROM THE PREVIOUS PAGE)

in Mukden without the approval of the civil government of Japan.

On the night of Sept. 18, 1931, Japanese troops used the pretext of an explosion along the Japanese-controlled South Manchurian Railway to occupy Mukden. On September 21, Japanese reinforcements arrived from Korea, and the army began to expand throughout northern Manchuria. In Tokyo neither the high command of the Japanese army nor Prime Minister Wakatsuki Reijirō proved able to restrain the Kwangtung Army in the field, and within three months Japanese troops had spread throughout Manchuria. Wakatsuki's cabinet fell in December, and its successor reacted to a growing tide of public opinion by sanctioning the invasion.

The Kwantung Army met little resistance in its conquests because Chiang Kai-shek, who was intent on establishing his control over the rest of China, ordered the commander of the Chinese forces in Manchuria, Zhang Xueliang, to pursue a policy of nonresistance and withdrawal. The League of Nations, Chiang announced, would determine the outcome of the case. The Lytton Commission, appointed by the league to investigate the situation, labeled Japan as the aggressor, but Japan withdrew from the league and continued to occupy Manchuria until 1945.

eliminated during the period of purges included two prime ministers, Peljidiin Genden (served 1932–36) and Anandyn Amar (1936–39), who after their arrest in Mongolia were tried in Moscow and executed (in 1937 and 1941, respectively) for "counterrevolutionary crimes"; Marshal Gelegdorjiin Demid, commander in chief of the army, who died of food poisoning while traveling on the Trans-Siberian Railway in August 1937; and Darizavyn Losol and Dansrangiin Dogsom, two veteran revolutionaries arrested in 1939 and sent to the Soviet Union, where Losol died in 1940 awaiting trial and Dogsom was executed in 1941.

Mongolia's slow collision with Japan escalated into a series of battles after the Japanese and Manchukuo troops invaded the northeastern corner of Mongolia in 1939. The fighting reached its climax in August, when Mongolian and Soviet troops under the command of Soviet Gen. Georgy Zhukov annihilated a large Japanese force near the Khalkhyn (Halhïn) River on the Mongolia-Manchukuo border. Japan subsequently abandoned any plans to invade the Soviet Union and shifted the focus of its expansionist efforts to the Pacific and Southeast Asia during World War II (1939–45).

Choibalsan, who in addition to serving as minister of internal affairs had become minister of war in 1937, was appointed the country's prime minister in March 1939. The MPRP congress held in March 1940 declared the beginning of the socialist stage of Mongolia's political development and named Yumjaagiin Tsedenbal general secretary of the party. Mongolia remained isolated from the outside world, recognized only by the Soviet Union, its political mentor and economic prop. Although Mongolia's health and education services had been greatly improved with Soviet help during the previous decade, industrial development was still in its infancy. The only major economic projects of the 1930s were a wool-washing factory set up at Lake Khövsgöl, a narrow-gauge railway line constructed between Ulaanbaatar and the nearby Nalaikh coal mine, and a complex of factories established at Ulaanbaatar that processed agricultural produce and made building materials.

In a major cultural change, it was agreed at a conference in Moscow in 1931 to create Latin scripts for the Mongol, Buryat, and Kalmyk languages. The plan was quickly implemented, with rules devised, publishing organized, teaching scheduled, and regulations issued. Official use began in 1933. However, Stalin later changed his mind; the Latin script was abandoned; and modified Cyrillic alphabets were ordered. The Cyrillic alphabet for

Mongol was introduced in 1945, and the traditional Mongolian vertical script was abandoned.

As World War II engulfed Europe, Japan signed a neutrality pact with the Soviet Union (April 1941). Two months later Nazi leader Adolf Hitler launched the German invasion of the Soviet Union, and Mongolia gave its Soviet ally moral support, material assistance (foodstuffs, livestock, and winter clothing), and later money to finance a tank regiment and a fighter squadron. At the Yalta Conference in February 1945, it was agreed that the Soviet Union would enter the war against Japan in exchange for recovering territory in the Far East previously lost to Japan and the understanding that the status quo in Mongolia's "independent" status (i.e., Soviet control) would be preserved. The Soviet Union and Mongolia declared war on Japan in early August and entered Inner Mongolia and Manchuria. By the time Japanese resistance had collapsed on August 22, Mongolian units had advanced southward beyond the Great Wall.

BETWEEN RUSSIA AND CHINA

As part of the Yalta Conference agreements, a plebiscite was held in Mongolia in October 1945 under

United Nations (UN) auspices, with the vote over-whelmingly in favour of independence over autono-my. The Republic of China recognized Mongolia in January 1946, and the two countries signed a friend-ship treaty in February. In June 1946 Mongolia made the first of several unsuccessful applications to join the UN. Meanwhile, Mongolia recognized the Peo-ple's Republic of China on the latter's proclamation in 1949 and established diplomatic relations with North Korea (1948), the Soviet satellite countries of eastern and central Europe (1950), and India (1955). Mongolia gained admission to the UN in 1961, and in 1963 the United Kingdom became the first West-ern country to establish relations with Mongolia.

The 1950s were a time of political transition and economic advancement. Choibalsan died in 1952 in a Moscow hospital, and Tsedenbal was appointed chairman (i.e., the equivalent of prime minister) of the Council of Ministers, (the highest organ of exec-utive power. In 1954 MPRP General Secretary Tsed-enbal was ousted by Dashiin Damba, who was des-ignated MPRP first secretary, but in 1958 Tsedenbal retook control of the party—also as first secretary—and had Damba dismissed on ideological grounds. The collectivization of livestock herding was com-pleted in the 1950s, as the herders were obliged to hand over all but a few of their animals to the large cooperative farms (*negdel*). The Trans-Mongolian Railway—jointly built by the Mongolians and Soviets and completed in 1955—spanned Mongolia from north to south and served as a symbol of Soviet-Chinese solidarity, but it was built using the Soviet broad rail gauge rather than the standard gauge used in China. In 1958 Mongolia began attending Comecon meetings, joining that organization in 1962.

Mongolia and China signed a treaty of friendship and mutual assistance in 1960, and the two countries amicably redemarcated the long frontier between them. However, the ideological dispute that developed between the Soviet Union and China over the unity and leadership of the communist movement soured Mongolia's relations with China. China sharply criticized the Soviets for their handling of the October 1962 Cuban missile crisis with the United States and two years later conducted its first atomic bomb test—the prevailing winds carrying radioactive fallout northward into Mongolian territory. In January 1966 Mongolia and the Soviet Union signed a new treaty of friendship, cooperation, and mutual assistance that included secret protocols allowing the Soviets to station troops, aircraft, and missiles in Mongolia. Sino-Soviet relations degenerated further following clashes between their troops along their border at the Ussuri (Wusuli) River in March 1969. Meanwhile, Chinese leader Mao Zedong had launched the movement that became known as the Cultural Revolution (1966–76), during which the Mongols of Inner Mongolia in particular suffered considerably.

In 1949 the MPRP had condemned how Mongolian history was being taught, claiming that those with "bourgeois nationalist" views were extolling Genghis Khan's conquests and Mongolia's "feudal" past at the expense of the achievements of the party and the Mongolian revolution. Nonetheless, as the 800th anniversary of Genghis Khan's birth approached in 1962, the party decided to organize celebrations honouring it that were to include unveiling a new monument to him, delivering speeches, and issuing a set of commemorative postage stamps. However, following Soviet criticisms that labeled Genghis a "reactionary" whose "Tatar-Mongol yoke" had laid waste to Russia, Mongolia quickly canceled the celebrations and withdrew the stamps. There followed a fresh MPRP evaluation of Genghis Khan, which also deemed him a reactionary and which credited him only for unifying the Mongol tribes. Any deviation from that line was considered unwanted promotion of nationalism and was not tolerated. This policy stifled virtually all discussion of Genghis Khan and Mongol nationalism for the next 40 years.

Tensions between Mongolia and China escalated throughout the 1970s. Mongolia accused China of wanting to annex Mongolia and, as a pretext for its territorial claims on Mongolian territory, of promoting Genghis Khan as a Yuan dynasty emperor. China, during its own 800th anniversary celebrations, countered by criticizing the Soviet Union for "occupying" Mongolia by stationing troops and military equipment there. In April 1978 China called for the Soviet withdrawal from Mongolia, and Premier Tsedenbal promptly visited a Soviet army unit stationed in Mongolia to thank it for protecting the country against the Chinese "threat." Mongolia began expelling Chinese immigrants in early 1979, accusing them of "expansionist plots," which further exacerbated distrust between the two countries. Tensions in the region eased considerably in the mid-1980s as Soviet and Mongolian leaders took steps to normalize relations with China. Diplomatic relations were restored between Mongolia and China in 1986.

CHAPTER FIVE

INDONESIA

••••••••••••••••••••••••••••

Indonesia was formerly known as the Dutch East Indies (or Netherlands East Indies). Although Indonesia did not become the country's official name until the time of independence, the name was used as early as 1884 by a German geographer; it is thought to derive from the Greek *indos*, meaning "India," and *nesos*, meaning "island." After a period of occupation by the Japanese (1942–45) during World War II, Indonesia declared its independence from the Netherlands in 1945. Its struggle for independence, however, continued until 1949, when the Dutch officially recognized Indonesian sovereignty. It was not until the United Nations (UN) acknowledged the western segment of New Guinea as part of Indonesia in 1969 that the country took on its present form.

EXPANSION OF EUROPEAN INFLUENCE

Although the presence of Portuguese traders in the archipelago was relatively unimportant in 16th-century Java, the fall of Malacca on the Malay Peninsula to the Portuguese in 1511 was a turning point in Indonesian history. By the end of the century, the level of Muslim Indonesian trade with the Middle East, and thence with Europe, was the greatest it had ever been. As commerce expanded, the Portuguese strove to secure control of trade with the Moluccas—the Spice Islands.

At the end of the 16th century, however, an increase in Dutch and British interests in the region gave rise to a series of voyages, including those of James Lancaster (1591 and 1601), Cornelis de Houtman and Frederik de Houtman (1595 and 1598), and Jacob van Neck (1598). In 1602 the Dutch East India Company (formal name United East India Company [Vereenigde Oost-Indische Compagnie; VOC]) received its charter, two years after the formation of the English East India Company. The VOC then inaugurated an effort to exclude European competitors from the archipelago—called the East Indies by Europeans. It also sought to control the trade carried on by indigenous Asian traders and to establish its own commercial monopoly.

Monopoly itself was not an innovation in the archipelago; Aceh, for example, had controlled trade on the northwest and east coasts of Sumatra. The company's monopoly, however, was more extensive and came to form the basis of the Dutch territorial empire. For these reasons many have tended to see either 1511 or the turn of the 17th century as the beginning of a period of European domination that lasted until the 20th century.

Since the 1930s, however, some historians have criticized the view that Europeans were the major factor in shaping the history of the East Indies from the 17th century onward. By contrast, they have stressed an essential continuity of Indonesian history and have argued that the VOC at first made little change in traditional political or commercial patterns. Traditional Asian commerce, according to one view, was a noncapitalistic peddling trade, financed by patrician classes in Asian countries and conducted by innumerable small traders who collected spices and pepper in the Indies for disposal in the port cities of Asia. In this view the VOC was seen, in effect, as merely another merchant prince, gradually inserting itself into the existing trade patterns of the Spice Islands and accommodating itself to them. As Batavia (now Jakarta) became the headquarters from which it established factories (trading posts) in the Spice Islands and elsewhere, the company gradually became a territorial power, but it was, at first, only one power among others and not yet ruler of the region. Only during the 19th century did new economic forces, the product of industrial capitalism, burst upon the islands and submerge them under a new wave of European imperialism.

GROWTH AND IMPACT OF THE DUTCH EAST INDIA COMPANY

Regardless of whether Europeans constituted the primary historical force in 17th-century Indonesia, their presence undoubtedly initiated changes that in the long run were to be of enormous importance. The VOC itself represented a new type of power in the region: it formed a single organization, traded across a vast area, possessed superior military force, and, in time, employed a bureaucracy of servants to look after its concerns in the East Indies. In sum, it could impose its will upon other rulers and force them to accept its trading conditions. Under the governor-generalship of Jan Pieterszoon Coen and his successors, particularly Anthony van Diemen (1636–45) and Joan Maetsuyker (1653–78), the company laid the foundations of the Dutch commercial empire and became the paramount power of the archipelago.

During the 17th century the VOC went far toward establishing commercial control in the Indonesian islands. It captured Malacca from the Portuguese (1641), confined the British—after a period of fierce rivalry—to a factory at Bencoolen (now Bengkulu), in southwestern Sumatra, and established a network of factories in the eastern islands. Though it may have wished to limit its activities to trade, the company was soon drawn into local politics in Java and elsewhere, and, in becoming the arbiter in dynastic disputes and in conflicts between rival rulers, it inevitably emerged as the main political entity in the archipelago.

In the 1620s Sultan Agung, ruler of the central Javanese kingdom of Mataram and representative of the old and highly sophisticated Javanese civilization, sought to extend his power over Bantam (near present-day Banten) in western Java. This brought him into conflict with the Dutch, and he laid siege to the Dutch fortress at Batavia. Although Agung's forces were eventually compelled to withdraw, the result of the confrontation was inconclusive and left both the Dutch and the Javanese warily respectful of each other's strength. Dutch intervention in Javanese affairs increased in the later 17th and early

This 17th-century engraving depicts Batavia, where the VOC was headquartered.

18th centuries, however, owing to internal dissensions within Mataram and a series of wars of succession between pretenders to the throne. In return for its services in 1674 to Amangkurat I, Sultan Agung's successor, and then to Amangkurat II shortly afterward, the VOC received the cession of the Preanger regions of western Java.

This was the first of a series of major territorial advances. In 1704 Dutch forces assisted in replacing Amangkurat III with his uncle, Pakubuwono I, in return for which further territory was ceded. In this way almost all of Java gradually came under Dutch control, and by 1755 only a remnant of the kingdom of Mataram remained. This was divided into two principalities, Yogyakarta (Jogjakarta) and Surakarta (Solo), which survived until the end of Dutch rule. In an attempt to control the pepper trade in Sumatra, the VOC established footholds in western Sumatra and in Jambi and Palembang over the course of the 17th century, and it interfered in local conflicts in support of rulers who favoured it. The main Dutch expansion in Sumatra did not take place until the 19th century, however.

In acquiring territorial responsibilities, the company did not at first establish a close administrative system of its own in the areas that were under its direct control. In effect, the VOC replaced the sovereign of the royal court and, in so doing, inherited the existing structure of authority. An indigenous aristocracy administered the collection of tribute on behalf of the company, and only gradually was this system converted into a formalized bureaucracy. The VOC, like the royal court before it, drew revenue in the form of produce from the peasantry within its domain.

To implement its commercial monopoly, the VOC established company factories for the collection of produce, pressured individual rulers to do business solely with the company, controlled the sources of supply of particular products (clove production, for example, was limited to Ambon, nutmeg and mace to the Banda Islands), and, in the 18th century, pushed through a system of forced deliveries and contingencies. Contingencies constituted a form of tax payable in kind in areas under the direct control of the company; forced deliveries consisted of produce that local cultivators were compelled to grow and sell to the company at a set price. There was little difference between the devices. In theory, forced deliveries were thought of as a form of trade in which goods were exchanged, but they were, in fact, as the British scholar J.S. Furnivall described it, "tribute disguised as trade," while contingencies were "tribute undisguised."

In effect, the whole system of company trade was designed to extract produce from the East Indies for disposal in a European market—but without stimulating any fundamental technological change in the area's economy. The profits belonged to the company, not to the producers. The indigenous traders of the region were pushed aside by the VOC as it gained control of more and more of the export trade of the archipelago. The growth of Batavia resulted, for example, in the decline of the north coast ports

THE FRENCH AND THE BRITISH IN JAVA, 1806–15

The fall of the Netherlands to France and the dissolution of the company led in due course to significant changes in the administration of the East Indies. Under Napoleon I the Batavian Republic became the Commonwealth of Batavia and then the Kingdom of Holland, with one of Napoleon's marshals, Herman Willem Daendels, serving as governor-general. Daendels strengthened Javanese defenses, raised new forces, built new roads within Java, and improved the internal administration of the island. He attempted to formalize the position of the Javanese regents, subordinating them to Dutch prefects and emphasizing their character as civil servants of a central government rather than as semi-independent local rulers.

In 1811 Java fell to a British East India Company force under Baron Minto, the governor-general of India, who, after the surrender, appointed Thomas Stamford Raffles lieutenant governor. Raffles approached his task with the conviction that British administrative principles, modeled in part on those developed in Bengal, could liberate the Javanese from the tyranny of Dutch methods; he believed that liberal economic principles and the cessation of compulsory cultivation could simultaneously expand Javanese agricultural production, improve revenue, and make the island a market for British goods. Along with his liberalism, Raffles brought to his task a respect for Javanese society. Before his appointment he had been a student of Malay literature and culture, and during his period in Batavia (Jakarta) he encouraged the study of the society he found about him. Raffles rediscovered the ruins of the great Buddhist temple Borobudur in central Java and published his *History of Java* in 1817, a year after his return to England.

Raffles carried further the administrative centralization begun by Daendels and planned to group the regencies of Java into 16 residencies. By declaring all lands the property of the government and by requiring cultivators to pay a land rent for its use, he proposed to end the compulsory production system. This, he believed, would free the peasants from servility to their "feudal"

(CONTINUED ON THE NEXT PAGE)

(CONTINUED FROM THE PREVIOUS PAGE)

rulers and from the burden of forced deliveries to the Dutch and allow them to expand their production under the stimulus of ordinary economic motives. Raffles oversimplified the complexities of traditional land tenure, however. He misread the position of the regents, whom he at first mistakenly believed to be a class of feudal landholders rather than an official aristocracy. (The regents, in fact, had no proprietary rights in the land of their subjects.) But despite a series of adjustments in his original plan, Raffles was unable to devise an effective means of applying his theories before the return of Java to Dutch hands as part of the general settlement following the defeat of Napoleon.

of Java, through which much of the spice trade had been channeled since before the 15th century. In this way the traditional pattern of trade was checked and distorted.

During the 18th century the VOC ran into financial difficulties from a variety of causes: the breach of the company's monopoly by smuggling, the growing administrative costs as the company came to shoulder greater responsibilities of government, and the corruption of the company's servants. Further complicating matters, the Netherlands (at the time, the Dutch Republic) succumbed to France during the French revolutionary wars and was restructured and renamed the Batavian Republic in 1795. In 1799 the (Dutch) government of the republic terminated the affairs of the Dutch East India Company.

DUTCH RULE FROM 1815 TO C. 1920

Before the 19th century, Indonesian societies had experienced considerable pressure from Europeans, but they had not been consumed by Western influences. The political order of Mataram had been eroded, and the first steps had been taken toward administrative centralization in Java. In the outer islands, local rulers had been forced to submit in some measure to the will of the Dutch headquartered in Batavia (Jakarta). The trading patterns of the archipelago had been changed and constricted. Nevertheless, these were superficial developments when seen against the continuing coherence and stability of Indonesian societies. They were superficial, also, compared with the Western impact still to come.

When the Dutch returned to Indonesia in 1815 after the Napoleonic Wars, their main concern was to make the colony self-supporting. During the interregnum, both exports and revenue had declined sharply, despite Raffles's hopes for his land-rent system. The costs of government in Java were rising as a result of the growing complexity of administration. In restoring their authority, the Dutch retained the main outlines of the British system of residencies, regencies, and lower administrative divisions, though they did not, at first, follow exactly the attempts of Daendels and Raffles to turn the regents into salaried officials, specifically responsible to the residents. Rather, they saw the local regent as the "younger brother" of the Dutch resident. This difference in theory was perhaps of slight practical effect, since the tendency in lower levels of territorial administration continued in the direction of an increasingly centralized control. Several factors contributed to the trend: one was the need to deal with a series of disturbances, primarily in Java and western Sumatra but also on a smaller scale in Celebes, Borneo, and the Moluccas; a second was the new economic policy, adopted in 1830, which increased the economic responsibilities of local officials.

The Java War of 1825–30 precipitated from a number of causes. In part, it was the product of the disappointed ambitions of its leader, Prince Diponegoro, who had been passed over for the succession to the throne of Yogyakarta. It was also attributable, however, to growing resentment among the aristocratic landholders of Yogyakarta, whose contracts for the lease of their lands to Europeans had been canceled by the governor-general. There was support too from Islamic leaders, as well as other hidden factors—such as the expectation of the coming of a messianic Just Ruler, who would restore the harmony of the kingdom—that undoubtedly added to the climate of discontent. From this agitated atmosphere erupted a revolt that, through the skillful use of guerrilla tactics, continued to challenge Dutch authority for five years, until the Dutch seized Diponegoro during truce negotiations and exiled him to Celebes.

About the same time, the Dutch in western Sumatra were drawn into the so-called Padri War (named for Pedir, a town in Aceh through which Muslim pilgrims usually returned home from Mecca). Basically, the war was a religious struggle in Minangkabau country between revivalist Islamic leaders (called Padris) and the local *adat* ("customary law") leaders, who were supported by the Dutch. Under Tuanku Imam Bonjol, the Padri forces resisted Dutch pressure from the early 1820s until 1837. For the Dutch the effect of this involvement was inevitably a strengthening of administrative commitment in western Sumatra.

THE CULTURE SYSTEM

The formation in 1824 of the Netherlands Trading Society (Nederlandsche Handel-Maatschappij; NHM)—a company embracing all merchants engaged in the East Indies trade and supported by the government of The Netherlands with the king as its chief shareholder—did not produce the hoped-for commercial expansion. In 1830, however, a newly appointed governor-general, Johannes van den Bosch, devised a new method by which the government could tap the resources of the archipelago. This was the so-called Culture System, or Cultivation System (*Cultuurstelsel*).

The Culture System provided that a village set aside a fifth of its cultivable land for the production of export crops. These crops were to be delivered to the government as land rent. Land rent, then, was the measure of the amount to be produced by each village. If a village, through the growing of export crops on a fifth of its land, returned an amount in excess of the land rent for which it had been assessed, it would be free of land rent and would be reimbursed to the extent of the excess; on the other hand, if a village produced less than the assessed amount of land rent, it would have to make up the difference.

A local Indonesian man is tried in a Dutch colonial court.

From the government's point of view, the Culture System was an overwhelming success. Exports soared, rising from 13 million guldens (the Dutch currency) in 1830 to 74 million a decade later. The products were disposed of through the Netherlands Trading Society, and between 1840 and 1880 their sale brought to the Dutch treasury an annual average of 18 million guldens, approximately a third of the Dutch budget.

The effects of the system for the Javanese were, however, of more dubious value. Though its founder believed that, by stimulating agricultural production, the Culture System would ultimately benefit the people of Java as well as the home government, it later came to be considered both by Dutch critics and by outside observers a particularly harsh and burdensome policy. Van den Bosch's expectations were not entirely false, however. The policy did extend village production in certain areas, and the population of Java increased from 6 million to 9.5 million during the full operation of the system. The range of exports from Java was broadened, and indigo and sugar were the first items to be made the subject of compulsory cultivation; coffee, tea, tobacco, and pepper were subsequently added.

Nevertheless, the system placed a heavy burden on the cultivators and tended to amplify social and economic inequities within rural society. Dominant peasants, members of a rural elite, were able to manipulate the system to their advantage. And while the Culture System brought the islands of the archipelago into contact with a wider overseas market, the East Indies government stood between producer and market, and the annual surplus added to Dutch, not Javanese, prosperity. The system did nothing to stimulate technological change or economic development for the Javanese people. An increasing commercial role was played not by the indigenous population but by Chinese immigrants, who fit into colonial rule as a separate caste, engaged in tax collection, money-lending, and small trading.

There were other consequences. The Culture System accentuated the differences between Java and the outer islands, and in Java it led to a considerable tightening of the administrative system. The regent became the kingpin of the system, responsible to the resident for the delivery of crops from his regency. Secure in the knowledge that they were backed by Dutch power, regents in some cases imposed additional burdens upon their subjects—a development that received trenchant criticism in the novel *Max Havelaar* (1860), written under the pseudonym Multatuli by the Dutch writer Eduard Douwes Dekker, a former official of the East Indies government. But the long-term effect of the new functions imposed on regents was to reduce their independence and to hasten the process, started by Daendels, by which a loosely structured administrative aristocracy was gradually converted into a salaried civil service. Regents were no longer able to draw their revenues from their subjects, and the lines of authority were clearly demarcated. Regents, aided by a junior Dutch official (the *controleur*), became clearly responsible to the Dutch residents above. By 1860 the administrative divisions of Java had been firmly established, and the service that staffed them had acquired the character it was essentially to preserve for the remainder of the colonial period.

In the 1860s the Culture System came under attack not only from humanitarian quarters but also from private business interests in The Netherlands. The latter appealed to liberal economic principles in support of their right to share in the riches of the East Indies; their pressure was effective. Although the Culture System was not abolished and continued for a number of years to make its contribution to the Dutch treasury, the decision was taken to encourage also the entry of private investment. The Liberal Policy, as it was called, was effectively inaugurated in 1870 by the adoption of an agrarian law that provided that European investors could acquire land under long-term leasehold, either from Indonesian landholders or, in the case of unoccupied land, from the government. Certain safeguards were provided for the Indonesian landholders: the provision that Europeans lease rather than purchase land was intended to prevent the alienation of Indonesian land, and the government was charged also with preventing Europeans from leasing land that was needed for the subsistence of village populations.

Within this framework Dutch capital began to flow to the East Indies on a scale that was to transform the character of the Indonesian economy and society. During the next 60 years there was a 10-fold increase in the value of exports (from 107 million guldens to 1.16 billion). There was a change also in kinds of products exported. Such exports as coffee, sugar, tea, and tobacco continued to expand, but such industrial raw materials as rubber, copra, tin, and oil soon came to dominate the export economy. These remarkable developments were in large measure the product of a totally different system of production. Under the company, during the interregnum, and, later, under the Dutch crown working through the Culture System, export crops were grown by Indonesian cultivators on their own land. Under the Liberal Policy, however, the new crops were the subject of estate production. Much economic expansion took place in Sumatra rather than Java, and Sumatra's east-coast residency became the seat of a vast new plantation economy. The estates were company-owned, and the economic developments of the late 19th century were indeed the product of corporate, rather than individual, enterprise.

DUTCH TERRITORIAL EXPANSION

Rapid economic development was accompanied by territorial expansion. Although the Dutch had established their control effectively over Java by the mid-18th century and had gradually expanded their original holdings in Sumatra over the course of the 19th, their control over the rest of the archipelago was patchy and incomplete. It was exercised, in the main, through agreements with local rulers rather than through direct control over territory. In the closing years of the 19th century and the early years of the 20th, rapid moves were made to round out the Dutch empire and extend it effectively over the whole of the East Indies.

In northern Sumatra, warfare with the people of Aceh that lasted with varying degrees of intensity from 1873 to 1908 brought the northern tip of Sumatra under Dutch control. In Celebes and the Moluccas, where the Dutch had long exercised a general authority, a new instrument—the Short Declaration (in contrast to the earlier Long Contract)—bound local rulers to accept the control of Batavia. Dutch authority was extended in this way over Bone and Luwu in the Celebes, over central Borneo, over Bali and the Lesser Sunda Islands, and over Ternate, Ceram, and Buru in the Moluccas. Footholds were established also over parts of western New Guinea. Communications were developed—roads and railways in Java and Sumatra and expanded shipping services to link Java to the outer islands—to serve the needs of the new plantation economy. Between 1870 and 1910 the Dutch had thus effectively completed the process of converting the East Indies into a unified colonial dependency and, indeed, of laying the foundations of the future Indonesian republic.

The "new imperialism" of the late 19th century may be seen as part of a worldwide movement whereby the industrial countries of western Europe partitioned among themselves the hitherto undeveloped areas of the globe. In Africa, in the South Pacific, and in Burma (Myanmar), Indochina, and Malaya, as well as in Indonesia, a new "forward movement" was taking place that stood in dramatic contrast to the earlier patterns of commercial empire. If the European presence created a veritable watershed in Indonesian history, it is to be discerned about 1870 (as opposed to 1511, which marked the establishment of a European base in the archipelago).

The social impact of these developments upon Indonesian society was tremendous. The economic and political expansion brought a new Dutch population to the East Indies: civil servants to staff the growing services of government, managers to run the new estates, and clerks to staff the import-export houses and other businesses. These new Dutch communities came to form European enclaves within the major cities, and their presence underscored the social divisions in what was increasingly a caste society divided along racial lines. The Dutch, however, were not merely a community of expatriates who were eager to retire as soon as possible to The Netherlands. Many of them regarded the East Indies as their home. Their sense of belonging was very different, for example, from that of the British in India, and it was to give an added bitterness to the later struggle to retain the colony after World War II.

From the Indonesian point of view, the growing cities became the home of a new urban way of life and stimulated social change. A new elite emerged under the influence of the expanding Western impact. So did a new class of unskilled and semiskilled workers who found employment as domestic servants or as labourers in the light industries that began to develop. Rural society, though more sheltered, was also altered by the currents of change. Although agrarian law and the later labour legislation had provisions to protect existing customary rights over land and to guarantee fairness of contracts for labourers, the mere fact of contract employment on the estates affected the village society from which workers were

drawn and played its part in hastening the growth
of a disoriented population, divorced increasingly
from the shelter of traditional village society but not
absorbed into the new urban culture.

THE ETHICAL POLICY

Dutch liberals confidently assumed that, just as freedom of enterprise would maximize welfare at home,
so the application of European capital to the task of
developing colonial resources would gradually improve the lot of colonial peoples. By the end of the
19th century, 30 years of the Liberal Policy in Indonesia did not appear to have achieved that miracle.
Growing criticism of the Dutch record in the East
Indies was given particularly influential expression by
Conrad Theodor van Deventer, a Liberal Democratic
member of the parliament of The Netherlands, who
argued that the Dutch had been draining wealth from
the East Indies and had incurred thereby a "Debt of
Honour" that should be repaid. His suggestion was
that The Netherlands turn from its strictly laissez-faire
policy in the East Indies to pursue instead a positive
welfare program supported by funds from the metro-
politan treasury. In 1901 a change of government in
The Netherlands provided the opportunity for a new
departure in policy along the lines suggested by van

Deventer. According to the Ethical Policy, as it was called, financial assistance from The Netherlands was to be devoted to the extension of health and education services and to the provision of agricultural extension services designed to stimulate the growth of the village economy.

The Ethical Policy was seen by its most fervent supporters as a noble experiment designed to transform Indonesian society, to enable a new elite to share in the riches of Western civilization, and to bring the colony into the modern world. Its ultimate goals were, of course, not clearly defined. Van Deventer looked to the emergence of a Westernized elite who would be "indebted to the Netherlands for its prosperity and higher Culture" and who would gratefully recognize the fact. Others hoped for the growth, by "cultural synthesis," of a new East Indian society based on a blending of elements of Indonesian and Western cultures and able to enjoy a large measure of autonomy within the framework of the Dutch empire.

Despite these rather grandiose visions, the achievements of the Ethical Policy were much more modest. It neither checked declining living standards nor promoted an agrarian revolution. It did provide agricultural assistance and advice, but this was directed to the improvement of techniques of irrigation and cultivation within the existing wet-rice technology of

Java. Its effect, therefore, was to confirm the gulf between the European economy of the estates, mines, oil wells, and large-scale commerce and the traditional, largely subsistence, Indonesian economy of wet-rice or shifting cultivation. In education a little was done to provide a greater degree of opportunity at primary, secondary, and even tertiary levels, but at the end of the 1930s only a handful of high school graduates were produced locally, and the literacy rate was calculated at just over 6 percent.

The goals of the Ethical Policy were set too high, and the devices adopted to implement them were too modest. Given the inertia of traditional societies, it was not to be expected that a new order would be created as easily as the proponents of the policy had hoped. Nevertheless, during the years of its operation, the East Indies were exposed to tremendous forces of social change. These forces, however, resulted not from the conscious plans of the Ethical Policy but from the undirected impact of Western economic development. Java's population, which had risen from about 6 million to almost 30 million over the course of the 19th century, increased to more than 40 million by 1920. The population increase, together with urbanization, the penetration of a money economy to the village level, and the labour demands of Western enterprise combined to disrupt traditional patterns.

Where the Ethical Policy was most effective, despite the limitations of its educational achievement, was in producing a small educated elite that could give expression to the frustration of the masses in a society torn loose from its traditional moorings. Western currents of thought had their impact also within Islamic circles, where modernist ideas sought to reconcile the demands of Islam and the needs of the 20th century. It is against this background that a self-conscious nationalist movement began to develop.

THE RISE OF NATIONALISM

Indonesian nationalism in the 20th century must be distinguished from earlier movements of protest; the Padri War, the Java War, and the many smaller examples of sporadic agrarian unrest had been "prenationalistic" movements, the products of local grievances. By contrast, the nationalism of the early 20th century was the product of the new imperialism and was part of wider currents of unrest affecting many parts of Africa and Asia that remained the subjects of Western colonialism. In Indonesia nationalism was concerned not merely with resistance to Dutch rule but with new perceptions of nationhood—embracing the ethnic diversity of the archipelago and looking to the restructuring of traditional patterns of authority in order to enable the creation of Indonesia as a modern state. It derived in part from specific discontents, the economic discriminations of colonial rule, the psychological hurt arising from the slights of social discrimination, and a new awareness of the all-pervading nature of Dutch authority. Important too was the emergence of the new elite, educated but lacking adequate employment opportunities to match that education, Westernized but retaining still its ties with traditional society.

Cut Nyak Dhien (*center*) was a leader of Acehnese guerrilla actions in the Aceh War (1873–1914). She was captured by the Dutch in 1905.

The formation in 1908 of Budi Utomo ("Noble Endeavour") is often taken as the beginning of organized nationalism. Founded by Wahidin Sudirohusodo, a retired Javanese doctor, Budi Utomo was an elitist organization, the aims of which—though cultural rather than political—included a concern to secure a mutual accommodation between traditional culture and contemporary society. Numerically more important was Sarekat Islam ("Islamic Association"), founded in 1912. Under its charismatic chairman, Omar Said Tjokroaminoto, the organization expanded rapidly, claiming a membership of 2,500,000 by 1919. Later research suggests that the real figure was likely to have been no more than 400,000, but even with this greatly reduced estimate, Sarekat Islam was clearly much larger than any other movement of the time.

In 1912 the Indies Party (Indische Partij)—primarily a Eurasian party—was founded by E.F.E. Douwes Dekker; banned a year later, it was succeeded by another Eurasian party, calling itself Insulinde, a poetic name for the East Indies. In 1914 the Dutchman Hendricus Sneevliet founded the Indies Social Democratic Association, which became a communist party in 1920 and adopted the name Indonesian Communist Party (Partai Komunis Indonesia; PKI) in 1924.

By the end of World War I, there had thus emerged a variety of organizations, broadly nationalist in aim, but differing in their tactics and immediate goals and in the sharpness of their perceptions of independent nationhood. In the absence of firm party discipline, it was common for individuals to belong simultaneously to more than one organization, and, in particular, the presence of Indies Social Democratic Association members in Sarekat Islam enabled them to work as a "bloc within" the larger movement. The idea that the time was not yet ripe for communist parties to assume independent leadership of colonial nationalism later led the Soviet-founded Communist International (also known Comintern or the Third International) to formulate the strategy of cooperation with anti-imperialist "bourgeois" parties.

At the end of World War I, the Dutch, in an effort to give substance to their promise to associate the Indonesian community more closely with government, created the People's Council (Volksraad). Composed of a mixture of appointed and elected representatives of the three racial divisions defined by the government—Dutch, Indonesian, and "foreign Asiatic"—the People's Council provided opportunities for debate and criticism but no real control over the government of the East Indies. Some nationalist leaders were prepared to accept seats in the assembly, but others refused, insisting that concessions could be obtained only through uncompromising struggle.

In 1921 the tension within Sarekat Islam between its more conservative leaders and the communists came to a head in a discipline resolution that insisted that members of Sarekat Islam belong to no other party; this, in effect, expelled the communist "bloc within," and there followed a fierce rivalry between the two for control of the grassroots membership of the organization. The PKI, once it had committed itself to independent action, began to move toward a policy of unilateral opposition to the colonial regime. Without the support of the Comintern, and even without complete unanimity within its own ranks, it launched a revolt in Java at the end of 1926 and in western Sumatra at the beginning of 1927. These movements, which had elements of traditional pro-test as well as of genuine communist insurrection, were easily crushed by the East Indies government, and communist activity was effectively ended for the remainder of the colonial period.

The defeat of the communist revolt and the ear-lier decline of Sarekat Islam left the way open for a new nationalist organization, and in 1926 a "general study club" was founded in Bandung, with a newly graduated engineer, Sukarno, as its secretary. The club began to reshape the idea of nationalism in a manner calculated to appeal to Indonesia's new ur-ban elite. After the failure of the ideologically based movements of Islam and communism, nationalist thinking was directed simply to the idea of a struggle for independence, without any precommitment to a particular political or social order afterward. Such a goal, it was believed, could appeal to all, including Muslims and communists, who could at least support a common struggle for independence, even if they differed fundamentally about what was to follow. Nationalism, in this sense, became the idea that the young Sukarno used as the basis of his attempt to unify the several streams of anticolonial feeling. The ideas of the Bandung Study Club were reinforced by currents of thought emanating from Indonesian students in The Netherlands. Their organization, restructured in 1924 under the self-consciously Indonesian (as opposed to Dutch) name Perhimpunan Indonesia (Indonesian Union), became a centre of radical nationalist thought, and in the mid-1920s students returning from The Netherlands joined forces with like-minded groups at home.

The new nationalism required a new organization for its expression, and in July 1927 the Indonesian Nationalist Association, later the Indonesian Nationalist Party (Partai Nasional Indonesia; PNI), was formed under the chairmanship of Sukarno. The PNI was based on the idea of noncooperation with the government of the East Indies and was thus distinguished from those groups, such as Sarekat Islam, that were prepared to accept People's Council membership. Sukarno, however, while seeking to create a basis of mass support for the PNI, also attempted with some success to work together with more-moderate leaders and succeeded in forming in the party a broadly based, if rather precarious, association of nationalist organizations.

The nationalist sentiment resonated beyond political parties, however. On Oct. 28, 1928, a number of representatives of youth organizations issued the historic Youth Pledge (Sumpah Pemuda), whereby they vowed to recognize only one Indonesian motherland, one Indonesian people, and one Indonesian language. It was a landmark event in the country's history and also is considered the founding moment of the Indonesian language.

At the end of 1929, Sukarno was arrested with some of his colleagues and was tried, convicted, and sentenced to four years in prison. He was released at the end of 1931, but by then the united movement he helped to create had begun to disintegrate. The PNI dissolved itself and reformed as Partindo. A number of other groups came together to form a new organization, the Indonesian National Education Club, known as the New PNI. While Partindo saw itself as a mass party on the lines of the old PNI, the New

PNI, under the leadership of Mohammad Hatta and Sutan Sjahrir, aimed at training cadres who could maintain continuing leadership of the movement should its leaders be arrested.

In 1933 Sukarno was arrested again and exiled to Flores; he later was transferred to Bengkulu in southern Sumatra. Repressive action followed against other party leaders, including Hatta and Sjahrir, who were also exiled. In the later 1930s nationalist leaders were forced to cooperate with the Dutch, and such moderate parties as Parindra accepted People's Council membership. In 1937 a more radical party, Gerindo, was formed, but it considered support of The Netherlands against the threat of National Socialism (Nazism) more important than the question of independence.

World War II changed the situation. The fall of the East Indies to Japan early in 1942 broke the continuity of Dutch rule and provided a completely new environment for nationalist activity.

JAPANESE OCCUPATION

Japanese military authorities in Java, having interned Dutch administrative personnel, found it necessary to use Indonesians in many administrative positions, which thus gave them opportunities that had been denied them under the Dutch. In order to secure popular acceptance of their rule, the Japanese sought also to enlist the support of both nationalist and Islamic leaders. Under this policy Sukarno and Hatta both accepted positions in the military administration.

Though initially welcomed as liberators, the Japanese gradually established themselves as overlords. Their policies fluctuated according to the exigencies of the war, but in general their primary object was to make the East Indies serve Japanese war needs. Nationalist leaders, however, felt able to trade support for political concessions. Sukarno was able to convince the administration that Indonesian support could be mobilized only through an organization that would represent genuine Indonesian aspirations. In March 1943 such an organization, Putera (Pusat Tenaga Rakjat; "Centre of the People's Power"), was inaugurated under his chairmanship. While the new organization enabled Sukarno to establish himself more clearly as the leader of the emergent country, and while it enabled him to develop more-effective lines of communication with the people, it also placed upon him the responsibility of sustaining Indonesian support for Japan through, among other devices, the *romusha* (forced-labour) program.

Later in the year Indonesian opinion was given a further forum in a Central Advisory Council and a series of local councils. At a different level, Indonesian youths were able to acquire a sense of group integrity through membership in the several youth organizations established by the Japanese. Of great importance also was the creation in October 1943 of a volunteer defense force composed of and officered by Indonesians trained by the Japanese. The Sukarela Tentara Pembela Tanah Air (Peta; "Volunteer Army of Defenders of the Homeland") would become the core military force of the Indonesian revolution.

In March 1944 the Japanese, feeling that Putera served Indonesian rather than Japanese interests, replaced it with a "people's loyalty organization" called Djawa Hokokai, which was kept under much closer control. Six months later the Japanese premier announced the Japanese intention to prepare the East Indies for self-government. In August 1945, on the eve of the Japanese surrender, Sukarno and Hatta were summoned to Saigon (now Ho Chi Minh City) in Vietnam, where Terauchi Hisaichi, commander of the Japanese expeditionary forces in Southeast Asia, promised an immediate transfer of independence.

On their return to Batavia (now Jakarta), Sukarno and Hatta were under pressure to declare independence unilaterally. This pressure reached its climax in the kidnapping of the two men, for a day, by some of Jakarta's youth leaders. On the morning of Aug.

17, 1945, after the news of the Japanese surrender had been confirmed, Sukarno and Hatta proclaimed Indonesia an independent republic.

THE REVOLUTION

The proclamation touched off a series of uprisings across Java that convinced the British troops entrusted with receiving the surrender of Japanese forces that the self-proclaimed republic was to be taken seriously. At the level of central government, the constitution adopted by the leaders of the new Republic of Indonesia was presidential in form, but the widely representative Central Indonesian National Committee became, in effect, an ad hoc parliament. Sukarno, as president, agreed to follow parliamentary conventions by making his cabinets dependent upon their ability to command the committee's confidence.

The spontaneous character of the Indonesian revolution was demonstrated by a number of incidents, notably the struggle for Bandung in late 1945 and early 1946 and the Battle of Surabaya in November 1945; in Surabaya Indonesian fighters resisted superior British forces for three weeks. Fighting also broke out in Sumatra and Celebes. Although the Dutch had expected to reassert their control over their colony without question, and although they

Revolutionary leader Sukarno was Indonesia's first president (1949–66).

were able to play upon the fears of the outer islands (generally, islands other than Java and Madura) of a Java-based republic, they eventually were compelled to negotiate with republican representatives led by Sjahrir, who by then was prime minister. The Linggadjati Agreement (drafted Nov. 15, 1946, and signed March 25, 1947), by which the Dutch agreed to transfer sovereignty in due course to a federal Indonesia, appeared to offer a solution to the conflict. (The Dutch claimed that a federation was necessary because of the diversity of the East Indies and the difference between heavily populated Java and the more sparsely populated outer islands.) Differing interpretations, however, made the agreement a dead letter from the beginning.

In July 1947 the Dutch, in an attempt to settle matters by force, initiated what they termed a police action against the republic. Its effect was to evoke United Nations (UN) intervention in the form of a commission known as the Good Offices Committee, and it ended in the precarious Renville Agreement of January 1948. In December 1948 a second police action was launched.

Meanwhile, the government of the republic faced some domestic opposition. In 1946 a left-wing plot was organized by followers of Ibrahim Datuk Tan Malaka, who opposed the policy of negotiation with the Dutch. This so-called July 3rd Affair was easily crushed. In September 1948 a more serious challenge, in the form of a communist revolt (the Madiun Affair), was also defeated.

The second police action aroused American concern. It also closed Indonesian ranks firmly behind the republic. In these circumstances The Netherlands, at a roundtable conference at The Hague, finally agreed in August 1949 to transfer sovereignty over its colony (with the exception of western New Guinea) to the independent United States of Indonesia in December 1949; a decision about the ultimate fate of western New Guinea was to be the subject of future negotiation.

CHAPTER SIX

PHILIPPINES

• •

The Philippines takes its name from Philip II, who was king of Spain during the Spanish colonization of the islands in the 16th century. Because it was under Spanish rule for 333 years and under U.S. tutelage for a further 48 years, the Philippines has many cultural affinities with the West. It is, for example, the second most-populous Asian country (following India) with English as an official language and one of only two predominantly Roman Catholic countries in Asia (the other being East Timor). Despite the prominence of such Anglo-European cultural characteristics, the peoples of the Philippines are Asian in consciousness and aspiration.

THE SPANISH PERIOD

Early Filipinos followed various local religions, a mixture of monotheism and polytheism in which the latter dominated. The propitiation of spirits required numerous rituals, but there was no obvious religious hierarchy. In religion, as in social structure and economic activity, there was considerable variation between—and even within—islands.

This pattern began to change in the 15th century, however, when Islam was introduced to Mindanao and the Sulu Archipelago through Brunei on the island of Borneo. Along with changes in religious beliefs and practices came new political and social institutions. By the mid-16th century two sultanates had been established, bringing under their sway a number of *barangay*s. A powerful *datu* as far north as Manila embraced Islam. It was in the midst of this wave of Islamic proselytism that the Spanish arrived. Had the Spanish come a century later or had their motives been strictly commercial, Filipinos today might be a predominantly Muslim people.

Spanish colonial motives were not, however, strictly commercial. The Spanish at first viewed the Philippines as a stepping-stone to the riches of the East Indies (Spice Islands), but, even after the Portuguese and Dutch had foreclosed that possibility, the Spanish still maintained their presence in the archipelago.

The Portuguese navigator and explorer Ferdinand Magellan headed the first Spanish foray to the

Philippines when he made landfall on Cebu in March 1521; a short time later he met an untimely death on the nearby island of Mactan. After King Philip II (for whom the islands are named) had dispatched three further expeditions that ended in disaster, he sent out Miguel López de Legazpi, who established the first permanent Spanish settlement, in Cebu, in 1565. The Spanish city of Manila was founded in 1571, and by the end of the 16th century most of the coastal and lowland areas from Luzon to northern Mindanao were under Spanish control. Friars marched with soldiers and soon accomplished the nominal conversion to Roman Catholicism of all the local people under Spanish administration. But the Muslims of Mindanao and Sulu, whom the Spanish called Moros, were never completely subdued by Spain.

Spanish rule for the first 100 years was exercised in most areas through a type of tax farming imported from the Americas and known as the *encomienda*. But abusive treatment of the local tribute payers and neglect of religious instruction by *encomenderos* (collectors of the tribute), as well as frequent withholding of revenues from the crown, caused the Spanish to abandon the system by the end of the 17th century. The governor-general, himself appointed by the king, began to appoint his own civil and military governors to rule directly.

In 1521 Ferdinand Magellan led the first Spanish expedition to the Philippines, which remained under Spanish rule for three centuries.

Central government in Manila retained a medieval cast until the 19th century, and the governor-general was so powerful that he was often likened to an independent monarch. He dominated the Audiencia, or high court, was captain-general of the armed forces, and enjoyed the privilege of engaging in commerce for private profit.

Manila dominated the islands not only as the political capital. The galleon trade with Acapulco, Mex., assured Manila's commercial primacy as well. The exchange of Chinese silks for Mexican silver not only kept in Manila those Spanish who were seeking quick profit, but it also attracted a large Chinese community. The Chinese, despite being the victims of periodic massacres at the hands of suspicious Spanish, persisted and soon established a dominance of commerce that survived through the centuries.

Manila was also the ecclesiastical capital of the Philippines. The governor-general was civil head of the church in the islands, but the archbishop vied with him for political supremacy. In the late 17th and 18th centuries the archbishop, who also had the legal status of lieutenant governor, frequently won. Augmenting their political power, religious orders, Roman Catholic hospitals and schools, and bishops acquired great wealth, mostly in land. Royal grants and devises formed the core of their holdings, but many arbitrary extensions were made beyond the boundaries of the original grants.

The power of the church derived not simply from wealth and official status. The priests and friars had a command of local languages rare among the lay Spanish, and in the provinces they outnumbered civil officials. Thus, they were an invaluable source of information to the colonial government. The cultural goal of the Spanish clergy was nothing less than the full Christianization and Hispanization of the Filipino. In the first decades of missionary work, local religions were vigorously suppressed; old practices were not tolerated. But as the Christian laity grew in number and the zeal of the clergy waned, it became increasingly difficult to prevent the preservation of ancient beliefs and customs under Roman Catholic garb. Thus, even in the area of religion, pre-Spanish Filipino culture was not entirely destroyed.

Economic and political institutions were also altered under Spanish impact but perhaps less thoroughly than in the religious realm. The priests tried to move all the people into pueblos, or villages, surrounding the great stone churches. But the dispersed demographic patterns of the old *barangay*s largely persisted. Nevertheless, the *datu*'s once hereditary position became subject to Spanish appointment.

Agricultural technology changed very slowly until the late 18th century, as shifting cultivation gradually gave way to more intensive sedentary farming, partly under the guidance of the friars. The socioeconomic consequences of the Spanish policies that accompanied this shift reinforced class differences. The *datu*s and other representatives of the old noble class took advantage of the introduction of the Western concept of absolute ownership of land to claim as their own fields cultivated by their various retainers, even though traditional land rights had been limited to usufruct. These heirs of pre-Spanish nobility were known as the *principalia* and played an important role in the friar-dominated local government.

THE 19TH CENTURY

By the late 18th century, political and economic changes in Europe were finally beginning to affect Spain and, thus, the Philippines. Important as a stimulus to trade was the gradual elimination of the monopoly enjoyed by the galleon to Acapulco. The last galleon arrived in Manila in 1815, and by the mid-1830s Manila was open to foreign merchants almost without restriction. The demand for Philippine sugar and abaca (hemp) grew apace, and the volume of exports to Europe expanded even further after the completion of the Suez Canal in 1869.

The growth of commercial agriculture resulted in the appearance of a new class. Alongside the landholdings of the church and the rice estates of the pre-Spanish nobility there arose haciendas of coffee, hemp, and sugar, often the property of enterprising Chinese-Filipino mestizos. Some of the families that gained prominence in the 19th century have continued to play an important role in Philippine economics and politics.

Not until 1863 was there public education in the Philippines, and even then the church controlled the curriculum. Less than one-fifth of those who went to school could read and write Spanish, and far fewer could speak it properly. The limited higher education in the colony was entirely under clerical direction, but by the 1880s many sons of the wealthy were sent to Europe to study. There, nationalism and a passion for reform blossomed in the liberal atmosphere. Out of this talented group of overseas Filipino students arose what came to be known as the Propaganda Movement. Magazines, poetry, and pamphleteering flourished. José Rizal, this movement's most brilliant figure, produced two political novels—*Noli me tangere* (1886; *Touch Me Not*) and *El filibusterismo* (1891; *The Reign of Greed*)—which had a wide impact in the Philippines. In 1892 Rizal returned home and formed the Liga Filipina, a modest reform-minded society, loyal to Spain, that breathed no word of independence. But Rizal was quickly arrested by the overly fearful Spanish, exiled to a remote island in the south, and finally executed in 1896. Meanwhile, within the Philippines there had developed a firm commitment to independence among a somewhat less privileged class.

Shocked by the arrest of Rizal in 1892, these activists quickly formed the Katipunan under the leadership of Andres Bonifacio, a self-educated warehouseman. The Katipunan was dedicated to the expulsion of the Spanish from the islands, and preparations were made for armed revolt. Filipino rebels had been numerous in the history of Spanish rule, but now for the first time they were inspired by nationalist ambitions and possessed the education needed to make success a real possibility.

THE PHILIPPINE REVOLUTION

In August 1896, Spanish friars uncovered evidence of the Katipunan's plans, and its leaders were forced into premature action. Revolts broke out in several provinces around Manila. After months of fighting, severe Spanish retaliation forced the revolutionary armies to retreat to the hills. In December 1897 a truce was concluded with the Spanish. Emilio Aguinaldo, a municipal mayor and commander of the rebel forces, was paid a large sum and was allowed to go to Hong Kong with other leaders; the Spanish promised reforms as well. But reforms were slow in coming, and small bands of rebels, distrustful of Spanish promises, kept their arms; clashes grew more frequent.

Meanwhile, war had broken out between Spain and the United States (the Spanish-American War). After the U.S. naval victory in the Battle of Manila Bay in May 1898, Aguinaldo and his entourage returned to the Philippines with the help of Adm. George Dewey. Confident of U.S. support, Aguinaldo reorganized his forces and soon liberated several towns south of Manila. Independence was declared on June 12 (now celebrated as Independence Day).

In September a constitutional congress met in Malolos, north of Manila, which drew up a fundamental law derived from European and Latin American precedents. A government was formed on the basis of that constitution in January 1899,

The Battle of Manila Bay on May 1, 1898, resulted in the fall of the Philippines. The U.S. Navy suffered fewer than 10 casualties; the Spanish Pacific fleet had 398.

with Aguinaldo as president of the new country, popularly known as the "Malolos Republic."

Meanwhile, U.S. troops had landed in Manila and, with important Filipino help, forced the capitulation in August 1898 of the Spanish commander there. The Americans, however, would not let Filipino forces enter the city. It was soon apparent to Aguinaldo and his advisers that earlier expressions of sympathy for Filipino independence by Dewey and U.S. consular officials in Hong Kong had little significance. They felt betrayed.

U.S. commissioners to the peace negotiations in Paris had been instructed to demand from Spain the cession of the Philippines to the United States; such cession was confirmed with the signing of the Treaty of Paris on Dec. 10, 1898. Ratification followed in the U.S. Senate in February 1899, but with only one vote more than the required two-thirds. Arguments of "manifest destiny" could not overwhelm a determined anti-imperialist minority.

By the time the treaty was ratified, hostilities had already broken out between U.S. and Filipino forces. Since Filipino leaders did not recognize U.S. sovereignty over the islands and U.S. commanders gave no weight to Filipino claims of independence, the conflict was inevitable. It took two years of counterinsurgency warfare and some wise conciliatory moves in the political arena to break the back of the nationalist resistance. Aguinaldo was captured in March 1901 and shortly thereafter appealed to his countrymen to accept U.S. rule.

The Filipino revolutionary movement had two goals, national and social. The first goal, independence, though realized briefly, was frustrated by the American decision to continue administering the islands. The goal of fundamental social change, manifest in the nationalization of friar lands by the Malolos Republic, was ultimately frustrated by the power and resilience of entrenched institutions. Share tenants who had rallied to Aguinaldo's cause, partly for economic reasons, merely exchanged one landlord for another. In any case, the proclamation of a republic in 1898 had marked the Filipinos as the first Asian people to try to throw off European colonial rule.

THE PERIOD OF U.S. INFLUENCE

The juxtaposition of U.S. democracy and imperial rule over a subject people was sufficiently jarring to most Americans that, from the beginning, the training of Filipinos for self-government and ultimate independence—the Malolos Republic was conveniently ignored—was an essential rationalization for U.S. hegemony in the islands. Policy differences between the two main political parties in the United States focused on the speed with which self-government should be extended and the date on which independence should be granted.

In 1899 Pres. William McKinley sent to the Philippines a five-person fact-finding commission headed by Cornell University president Jacob G. Schurman. Schurman reported back that Filipinos wanted ultimate independence, but this had no immediate impact on policy. McKinley sent out the Second Philippine

Commission in 1900, under William Howard Taft; by July 1901 it had established civil government.

In 1907 the Philippine Commission, which had been acting as both legislature and governor-general's cabinet, became the upper house of a bicameral body. The new 80-member Philippine Assembly was directly elected by a somewhat restricted electorate from single-member districts, making it the first elective legislative body in Southeast Asia. When Gov.- Gen. Francis B. Harrison appointed a Filipino majority to the commission in 1913, the American voice in the legislative process was further reduced.

The democratically elected Philippine Assembly first met in 1907.

Harrison was the only governor-general appointed by a Democratic president in the first 35 years of U.S. rule. He had been sent by Woodrow Wilson with specific instructions to prepare the Philippines for ultimate independence, a goal that Wilson enthusiastically supported. During Harrison's term, a Democratic-controlled Congress in Washington, D.C., hastened to fulfill long-standing campaign promises to the same end. The Jones Act, passed in 1916, would have fixed a definite date for the granting of independence if the Senate had had its way, but the House prevented such a move. In its final form the act merely stated that it was the "purpose of the people of the United States" to recognize Philippine independence "as soon as a stable government can be established therein." Its greater importance was as a milestone in the development of Philippine autonomy. Under Jones Act provisions, the commission was abolished and was replaced by a 24-member Senate, almost wholly elected. The electorate was expanded to include all literate males.

Some substantial restrictions on Philippine autonomy remained, however. Defense and foreign affairs remained exclusive U.S. prerogatives. American direction of Philippine domestic affairs was exercised primarily through the governor-general and the executive branch of insular government. There was little more than one decade of thoroughly U.S. administration in the islands, however—too short a time in which to establish lasting patterns. Whereas Americans formed 51 percent of the civil service in 1903, they were only 29 percent in 1913 and 6 percent in 1923. By 1916 Filipino dominance in both the legislative and judicial branches of government also served to restrict the U.S. executive and administrative roles.

By 1925 the only American left in the governor-general's cabinet was the secretary of public instruction, who was also the lieutenant governor-general. This is one indication of the high priority given to education in U.S. policy. In the initial years of U.S. rule, hundreds of schoolteachers came from the United States. But Filipino teachers were trained so rapidly that by 1927 they constituted nearly all of the 26,200 teachers in public schools. The school population expanded fivefold in a generation; education consumed half of governmental expenditures at all levels, and educational opportunity in the Philippines was greater than in any other colony in Asia.

As a consequence of this pedagogical explosion, literacy doubled to nearly half in the 1930s, and educated Filipinos acquired a common language and a linguistic key to Western civilization. By 1939 some one-fourth of the population could speak English, a larger proportion than for any of the native dialects. Perhaps more important was the new avenue of upward social mobility that education offered. Educational policy was the only successful U.S. effort to establish a sociocultural basis for political democracy.

American attempts to create equality of economic opportunity were more modest and less successful. In a predominantly agricultural country the pattern of landownership is crucial. The trend toward greater concentration of ownership, which began in the 19th century, continued during the American period, despite some legal barriers. Vast American-owned plantations were forestalled, but legal restrictions had little effect on those politically well-connected Filipinos who were intent on amassing fortunes. The percentage of farmers under share tenancy doubled between 1900 and 1935, and the frustration of the tenants erupted in three small rebellions in central Luzon during the 1920s and '30s.

Nor was U.S. trade policy conducive to the diffusion of economic power. From 1909 the Payne-Aldrich Tariff Act allowed free entry of Philippine products into the U.S. market, at the same time U.S. products, mostly manufactured, were exempted from tariff in the Philippines. The free flow of U.S. imports was a powerful deterrent to Philippine industrial growth. Export agriculture, especially sugar, prospered in the protected U.S. market. Owners of mills and large plantations profited most, thus reinforcing the political dominance of the landed elite.

American preparation of the Philippines for democratic self-government suffered from an inherent contradiction, perhaps not recognized at the time. Transferring governmental responsibility to those capable of undertaking it was not consistent with building a social and economic base for political democracy. Self-government meant, of necessity, assumption of power by those Filipinos who were already in positions of leadership in society. But those men came for the most part from the landed elite; preservation of their political and economic position was incompatible with equalizing opportunity. Even the expansion of an educated middle class did not necessarily result in a transformation of the pattern of power. Most middle-class aspirants for political leadership adjusted to the values and the practices of the existing power elite.

Filipino leaders quickly and skillfully utilized the opportunities for self-government that the Americans opened to them. The Filipino political genius was best reflected in an extralegal institution—the political party. The first party, the Federal Party, was U.S.-backed and stressed cooperation with the overlords, even to the point of statehood for the Philippines. But when openly nationalist appeals were allowed in the 1907 election, the Nacionalista Party, advocating independence, won overwhelmingly. The Federalists survived with a new name, Progressives, and a new platform, ultimate independence after social reform. But neither the Progressives nor their successors in the 1920s, the Democrats, ever gained more than one-third of the seats in the legislature. The Nacionalista Party under the leadership of Manuel Quezon and Sergio Osmeña dominated Philippine politics from 1907 until independence.

More significant than the competition between the Nacionalistas and their opposition was the continuing rivalry between Quezon and Osmeña. In fact, understanding this personality conflict provides more insight into the realities of prewar Philippine politics than any examination of policy or ideology.

In 1933 the U.S. Congress passed the Hare-Hawes-Cutting Act, which set a date for Philippine independence. The act was a fulfillment of the vague pledge in the Jones Act; it was also responsive to the demands of a series of "independence missions" sent to Washington by the Philippine legislature. But this unprecedented transfer of sovereignty was decided upon in the dark days of the Great Depression of the 1930s—and with the help of some incongruous

Manuel Quezon was a Filipino statesman, leader of the independence movement, and first president of the Philippine Commonwealth established under U.S. tutelage in 1935.

allies. The Depression had caused American farm interests to look desperately for relief, and those who suffered real or imaginary hurt from the competition of Philippine products sought to exclude those products. They had already failed in a direct attempt to amend the tariff on Philippine imports but found that the respectable cloak of the advocacy of independence increased the effectiveness of their efforts. Tied to independence was the end of free entry into American markets of Philippine sugar, coconut oil, rope, and other less important items. That those economic interests were able to accomplish what they did is partly explainable by the fact that their political clout was great compared with that of the small group of American traders and investors in the Philippines.

The Philippine legislature rejected the Hare-Hawes-Cutting Act, apparently as a result of the Osmeña-Quezon feud, much to the displeasure of American officialdom. But, when Quezon came to Washington the following year to work for a new bill, the same alliance of forces in the U.S. Congress obliged by producing the almost identical Tydings-McDuffie Act. Endorsed by Quezon and accepted with alacrity by the Manila legislature, it provided for a 10-year commonwealth during which the U.S. would retain jurisdiction over defense and foreign affairs. Filipinos were to draft their own constitution, subject to the approval of the U.S. president.

A constitutional convention was quickly elected and a constitution (which bore a strong resemblance to its U.S. model) framed and approved by plebiscite and by Pres. Franklin D. Roosevelt. The last governor-general, Frank Murphy, became the first high commissioner, with more of a diplomatic than a governing role. The commonwealth was inaugurated on Nov. 15, 1935. The Nacionalista Party patched up its internal quarrels and nominated Quezon for president and Osmeña for vice president. They were elected overwhelmingly.

The commonwealth period was intended to be devoted to preparation for economic and political independence and perfection of democratic institutions. But even before the tragic events of World War II, the transition did not run smoothly.

WORLD WAR II

Japanese aggression in China prompted much attention to military preparedness. Nearly one-fourth of the national budget was devoted to defense. Gen. Douglas MacArthur, retiring as army chief of staff in Washington, was called by President Quezon to direct plans and preparations. Meanwhile, agrarian unrest festered, and leftist political activity grew. Quezon pushed significant reform legislation through the National Assembly, but implementation was feeble, despite the rapid accumulation of power in his hands.

The Japanese attack of the Philippines on Dec. 8, 1941, came at a time when the U.S. military buildup had hardly begun. Their advance was rapid; before Christmas, Manila was declared an "open city," while Quezon and Osmeña were evacuated to MacArthur's headquarters on Corregidor Island. Despite a desire, at one point, to return to Manila in order to surrender, Quezon was persuaded to leave the Philippines in March 1942 on a U.S. submarine; he was never to return. Osmeña also went. Filipino and American forces, under Gen. Jonathan M. Wainwright, surrendered in May. An Executive Commission made up of more than 30 members of the old Filipino political elite had been cooperating with Japanese military authorities in Manila since January.

The Executive Commission lasted until September 1943, when it was superseded by an "independent Philippine Republic." The president, chosen by the Japanese, was José Laurel, former associate justice of the commonwealth Supreme Court and the only Filipino to hold an honorary degree from Tokyo

Imperial University. More than half of the commonwealth Senate and more than one-third of the House
served at one time in the Japanese-sponsored regime.
Yet collaboration with Japan was neither as willing
nor as widespread as elsewhere in Southeast Asia.

Even before the fall of Bataan Peninsula to the
Japanese in April 1942, guerrilla units were forming throughout the Philippines. Most were led by
middle-class officers and were enthusiastically
pro-United States; in central Luzon, however, a
major force was the Hukbalahap, which, under communist leadership, capitalized on earlier agrarian unrest. Though in a number of instances collaborators
secretly assisted guerrillas, many guerrillas in the
hills were bitter against those who appeared to benefit from the occupation. The differences between
the two groups became an important factor in early
postwar politics.

Soon after the U.S. landings on Leyte in October 1944, commanded by MacArthur, civil government was returned to the commonwealth, at least in
name. Sergio Osmeña, who had become president
in exile on the death of Quezon in August, had few
resources to deal with the problems at hand, however. Osmeña's role was complicated by the fact
that MacArthur chose to lionize Manuel A. Roxas,
a leading collaborator who had also been in contact

with U.S. military intelligence. As president of the Senate, Roxas became, in effect, MacArthur's candidate for president. Roxas was nominated in January 1946 in a separate convention of the "liberal wing" of the Nacionalista Party, as it was first called. Thus was born the Philippines' second major political party, the Liberals.

Osmeña, though he had the advantages of incumbency, was old and tired and did not fully use the political tools he possessed. In April Roxas was elected by a narrow margin. The following month he was inaugurated as the last chief executive of the commonwealth, and on July 4, 1946, when the Republic of the Philippines was proclaimed, he became its first president.

THE EARLY REPUBLIC

Roxas, as expected, extended amnesty to all major collaborators with Japan. In the campaign for the election of 1949 there was an attempt to raise the collaboration issue against José Laurel, the Nacionalista presidential candidate, but it was not effective. In the fluidity of Philippine politics, "guerrillas" and "collaborators" were by that time to be found on both sides of all political fences.

The Philippines had gained independence in the "ashes of victory." Intense fighting, especially around Manila in the last days of the Japanese retreat (February–March 1945), had nearly destroyed the capital. The economy generally was in disarray. Rehabilitation aid was obviously needed, and President Roxas was willing to accept some onerous conditions placed implicitly and explicitly by the U.S. Congress. The Bell Act in the United States extended free trade with the Philippines for 8 years, followed by 20 years of gradually increasing tariffs. The United States demanded and received a 99-year lease on a number of Philippine military and naval bases in which U.S. authorities had virtual territorial rights. And finally, as a specific requirement for release of U.S. war-damage payments, the Philippines had to amend its constitution to give U.S. citizens equal rights with Filipinos in the exploitation of natural resources—the so-called Parity Amendment.

The changing character of Philippine–U.S. relations was a major theme in Philippine history for the first several decades after the war. The trend was toward weakening of the link, achieved partly by diversifying Philippine external ties and partly by more articulate anti-American feeling. Economic nationalism, though first directed against the local Chinese community's dominance of retail trade, by the 1950s was focused on the special status of American business firms.

At independence the military ties with the United States were as strong as the economic ones. Filipino troops fought against communist forces in Korea, and noncombatant engineers augmented U.S. forces in the Vietnam War. Crucial to U.S. military action in Vietnam were bases in the Philippines. The Military Bases Agreement was the greatest single cause of friction in relations between the United States and the Philippines. Beginning in 1965, however, a series of agreements between the two countries reduced the size and number of the U.S. bases and shortened base leases. In 1979 formal jurisdiction over the base areas passed to the Philippine government; and the constitution of 1987 formalized the process by which the bases agreement could be extended beyond the expiration in 1991 of base leases. Extension of the agreement was ultimately rejected by the Philippine Senate, however, and U.S. forces were pulled from the Philippine bases in 1992.

The nature and effectiveness of Filipino political institutions since independence has been a special concern of the former colonial power that helped establish them. For Filipinos, those institutions have determined the ability or inability to maintain domestic social order. Clumsy repression of dissent and the fraudulent election of the country's second president, Elpidio Quirino, in 1949 set the stage for

THE HUKBALAHAP REBELLION

The Hukbalahap Rebellion, also called the Huk Rebellion, was a Communist-led peasant uprising in central Luzon, Philippines, that lasted from 1946 until 1954. The name of the movement is a Tagalog acronym for Hukbo ng Bayan Laban sa Hapon, which means "People's Anti-Japanese Army." The Huks came close to victory in 1950 but were subsequently defeated by a combination of advanced U.S. weaponry supplied to the Philippine government and administrative reforms under the charismatic Philippine president Ramon Magsaysay.

The central Luzon plain is a rich agricultural area where a large peasant population worked as tenant farmers on vast estates. The visible contrast between the wealthy few and the poverty-stricken masses was responsible for periodic peasant revolts during the Spanish period of Philippine history. During the 1930s central Luzon became a focus for Communist and Socialist organizational activities.

(CONTINUED ON THE NEXT PAGE)

(CONTINUED FROM THE PREVIOUS PAGE)

World War II brought matters to a head. Unlike many other Southeast Asians, the Filipinos offered strong resistance against the Japanese. After the fall of Bataan to the Japanese (April 1942), organized guerrilla bands carried on the fight for the remainder of the occupation period. The Hukbalahap organization proved highly successful as a guerrilla group and killed many Japanese troops. The Huks regarded wealthy Filipinos who collaborated with the Japanese as fair targets for assassination, and by the end of the war they had seized most of the large estates in central Luzon. They established a regional government, collected taxes, and administered their own laws.

The returning U.S. Army was suspicious of the Huks because of their Communist leadership. Tension between the Huks and the Philippine government immediately arose over the issue of surrender of arms. The Huks had gathered an estimated 500,000 rifles and were reluctant to turn them over to a government they regarded as oligarchic.

Philippine independence from the United States was scheduled for July 4, 1946. An election was held in April for positions in the new government. The Hukbalahap participated, and the Huk leader Luis Taruc won a seat in Congress but—along with some other Huk candidates—was unseated by the victorious Liberal Party. The Huks then retreated to the jungle and began their rebellion. Immediately after independence, Philippine president Manuel Roxas announced his "mailed fist" policy toward the Huks. The morale of government troops was low, however, and their indiscriminate retaliations against villagers only strengthened Huk appeal. During the next four years, the Manila government steadily slipped in prestige while Huk strength increased. By 1950 the guerrillas were approaching Manila, and the Communist leadership decided the time was ripe for a seizure of power.

The Huks suffered a crucial setback when government agents raided their secret headquarters in Manila. The entire Huk political leadership was arrested in a single night. At the same time, Huk strength was dealt another blow when U.S. President Harry Truman, alarmed at the worldwide expansion of Communist power, authorized large shipments of military supplies to the Manila government.

(CONTINUED ON THE NEXT PAGE)

(*CONTINUED FROM THE PREVIOUS PAGE*)

Another factor in the Huk defeat was the rise to power of the popular Ramon Magsaysay. His election as president in 1953 signaled a swing of popular support back to the Manila government. In 1954 Taruc emerged from the jungle to surrender, and the Hukbalahap Rebellion, for all practical purposes, came to an end.

The Huk movement and its leadership persisted, however, operating primarily from a stronghold in Pampanga province on Luzon Island. With the failure of subsequent Philippine administrations to implement the long-promised land reforms, the Huks—although split into factions and, in some areas, merged with new insurgent groups—continued into the 1970s as an active antigovernment organization.

an intensification of the communist-led Hukbalahap (Huk) Rebellion, which had begun in 1946. The rebellion also reflected a growing sense of social injustice among tenant farmers, especially in central Luzon. Suppression of the rebellion five years later, however, was attributable to American military aid as well as to the opening of the political process to greater mass participation, particularly during the campaign of Ramon Magsaysay, a uniquely charismatic figure in Filipino politics who was elected president in 1953. Magsaysay's attempts at social and economic reform failed largely because of the conservative outlook of the legislature and the bureaucracy. When Magsaysay died in a plane crash in 1957, leadership of the country fell to his vice president, Carlos P. Garcia. During Garcia's presidential term and that of his reform-minded successor, Diosdado Macapagal (1961–65), unrest was usually channeled through the electoral process and peaceful protest.

CHAPTER SEVEN

MALAYSIA AND MYANMAR

• •

The modern countries of Malaysia and Myanmar (former Burma) were both under British rule until the mid-20th century. Malaysia is composed of two noncontiguous regions: Peninsular Malaysia (Semenanjung Malaysia), also called West Malaysia (Malaysia Barat), which is on the Malay Peninsula, and East Malaysia (Malaysia Timur), which is on the island of Borneo. Malaysia, a member of the Commonwealth, represents the political marriage of territories that were formerly under British rule. The country now known as Myanmar was known as Burma beginning in 1885, when Britain established rule over it. Burma became an independent republic in 1948 and formally changed its name to the Union of Myanmar in 1989.

MALAYSIA

The fame of Malacca as the crossroads of Asian commerce had reached Europe by the beginning of the 16th century. The Portuguese, who for a century had been seeking a sea route to eastern Asia, finally arrived at Malacca in 1509, inaugurating a new era of European activity in Southeast Asia. Although much of Southeast Asia, including northern Borneo, experienced little Western impact before the 19th century, Malaya was one of the first regions to be disrupted. In 1511 a Portuguese fleet led by Afonso de Albuquerque captured Malacca.

Malacca, seen in this 18th-century Dutch engraving, was an important trade port in Southeast Asia.

EARLY EUROPEAN INTRUSIONS AND EMERGING SULTANATES

Because few merchants of Malacca chose to endure the conquerors' high taxes and intolerance of Islam, the city ultimately languished under Portuguese control. The sultanate of Aceh (Acheh) in northern Sumatra subsequently leaped into the political vacuum created by Malacca's decline, and during the 16th and early 17th centuries the Acehnese were deeply involved in peninsular affairs, warring against various sultanates and at times controlling some or most of them. Indeed, the understaffed Portuguese authority in Malacca was barely able to repulse repeated assaults by the sultanate of Aceh. Meanwhile, the Dutch, having established the Dutch East India Company in 1602, arose as the dominant European power in Southeast Asia. In 1641 the Dutch seized Malacca, and although they tried to revive its trade, the city never recovered its earlier glory.

Throughout the rise and fall of Malacca, new sultanates were emerging elsewhere in the Malay world. They usually were situated at the mouth of a major river and sought to control trade to and from the interior, which often was populated by seminomadic peoples such as the aboriginal Orang Asli ("Original People") of Malaya and the various indigenous peoples of Borneo. Younger sultanates—such as Riau-Johor and Kedah, both on the peninsula, and Brunei, on Borneo's northern coast—took over some of the trading functions of Malacca and flourished for several centuries. Islam reached other areas of northern Borneo in the 15th and 16th centuries; many coastal peoples converted, but most of the inhabitants of the interior continued to practice local religions well into the 20th century.

Malay political control spread, with the Brunei sultans laying claim to much of what are today Sarawak and Sabah—although their actual power seldom reached much beyond the coastal zone. Attempts by Brunei to control the interior often failed, especially after the aggressive Iban (Sea Dayak) people commenced their migrations into present-day Sarawak from western Borneo (16th through 18th centuries). The Siamese came to control some of the northern Malay sultanates, and the southernmost part of present-day Thailand still has a predominantly Malay Muslim population. The Malay sultanates included many, often feuding chiefdoms. Consequently, wars within and between the sultanates erupted from time to time. From the Europeans' perspective, the sultanate system—with its hierarchical but fluctuating spheres of influence over mobile populations—was politically unstable.

During the 17th century many Minangkabau people migrated from western Sumatra into southwestern Malaya, bringing with them a matrilineal sociocultural system by which property and authority descended through the female side. They elected their chiefs from among eligible aristocratic candidates, a model that has been incorporated into contemporary Malaysia's selection of a king. Later the Minangkabau formed a confederation of nine small states (Negeri Sembilan). The political pluralism of Malaya in the 18th century also facilitated large-scale penetration of the peninsula by Buginese people from southwestern Celebes (Sulawesi), a large island to the southeast of Borneo that is now part of Indonesia. With a well-earned reputation as maritime traders, Buginese immigrants established the sultanate of Selangor on the west coast of Malaya in the mid-1700s. To the southeast, they gained prominence in the sultanate of Johor, which, at the tip of the peninsula, was a prosperous trading entrepôt that attracted Asian and European merchants.

Despite continuous movement of peoples from the archipelago into the area, Malaya and northern Borneo remained sparsely populated into the early 19th century. Many present-day Malays are descendants of immigrants from elsewhere in archipelagic Southeast Asia who arrived after 1800.

Indeed, immigrants from Java, Celebes, and Sumatra demonstrated a tendency to assimilate to the existing Malay community over time, a process that steadily accelerated with the rise of Malay nationalism and vernacular education in the 1930s. Some of the traditions brought by Minangkabau, Javanese, and other immigrants are still practiced in districts where they settled, contributing to the many regional variations of Malay culture and language.

MALAYA AND NORTHERN BORNEO UNDER BRITISH CONTROL

Except for Malacca, Western influence was negligible in Malaya and northern Borneo until the late 18th century, when Britain became interested in the area. The British sought a source for goods to be sold in China, and in 1786 the British East India Company acquired the island of Penang (Pulau Pinang), off Malaya's northwest coast, from the sultan of Kedah. The island soon became a major trading entrepôt with a chiefly Chinese population. British representative Sir Stamford Raffles occupied the island of Singapore off the southern tip of the peninsula in 1819 and acquired trading rights in 1824; a strategic location at the southern end of the Strait of Malacca and a fine harbour made Singapore the centre for

Britain's economic and political thrust in the peninsula. The British attracted Chinese immigrants to the sparsely populated island, and soon the mainly Chinese port became the region's dominant city and a major base for Chinese economic activity in Southeast Asia. By then the predominant industrial capitalist power in Europe, Britain next obtained Malacca from the Dutch in 1824 and thereafter governed the three major ports of the Strait of Malacca—Penang, Malacca, and Singapore—which collectively were called the Straits Settlements. The British Colonial Office took direct control in 1867.

With the opening in 1869 of the Suez Canal, which provided a dramatically shorter maritime route between Europe and Southeast Asia, the full effect of European technological development swept over the region. The feuding Malay states were little prepared for the political ramifications of increased European commercial activity, with the exception of Johor, which was led by the strong, shrewd, and progressive sultan Abu Bakar. The other state administrations generally were weak and failed to cope with their mounting problems, including the steady immigration of Chinese.

By the early 19th century the Chinese—who were being driven to emigrate by increasing poverty and instability in their homeland—began settling in large numbers in the sultanates along the peninsula's west coast, where they cooperated with local Malay rulers to mine tin. The Chinese organized themselves into tightly knit communities and formed alliances with competing Malay chiefs, and Chinese factions fought wars with each other for control of minerals. Chinese settlers also established towns such as Kuala Lumpur and Ipoh, which later grew into major cities. The Chinese and Malays increasingly became entrenched in an inadequately integrated sociopolitical structure that continually generated friction between the two communities.

British investors were soon attracted to Malaya's potential mineral wealth, but they were concerned about the political unrest. As a result, by the 1870s local British officials began to intervene in the internal affairs of various Malayan sultanates—establishing political influence (sometimes by force or the threat of force) through a system of British residents (advisers). Initial intervention was crude and incompetent; the first British resident to Perak was murdered by Malays outraged by his assertive actions. Gradually, the British refined their techniques and appointed more-able representatives; notable among these was Sir Frank Swettenham, who in 1896 became the first resident-general of a Malay federation of Perak, Selangor, Negeri Sembilan, and Pahang, with Kuala Lumpur as the capital. By 1909 the British had pressured Siam (now Thailand) into transferring sovereignty over the northern Malay states of Kedah, Terengganu, Kelantan, and Perlis; Johor was compelled to accept a British resident in 1914. These five sultanates remained outside the Malay federation, however. Britain had now achieved formal or informal colonial control over nine sultanates, but it pledged not to interfere in matters of religion, customs, or the symbolic political role of the sultans. The various states kept their separate identities but were increasingly integrated to form British Malaya.

Sarawak also entered a new historical era when the English adventurer James (later Sir James) Brooke helped the sultan of Brunei suppress a local revolt by several Iban groups that (theoretically) were under the sultanate's control. In gratitude, the sultan of Brunei appointed Brooke raja (governor) of the Sarawak River basin in 1841. Brooke inaugurated not only a new form of imperial endeavour but also a century of rule by successive generations of a remarkable English family—a dynasty known as the Brooke Raj. As traditional Bornean rulers, generally benevolent autocrats, and cautious modernizers, the Brookes viewed themselves as protectors of Sarawak's people. James Brooke spent the years before his death in 1868 consolidating his control of surrounding districts and defending his government against various challenges.

Sarawak acquired the status of an independent state under British protection during the reign of its second raja, Charles Brooke (nephew of James Brooke). Relations with Britain, however, were often strained, chiefly because of a consistent Brooke policy of incorporating territory at the expense of the declining Brunei sultanate, which also became a British protectorate in the late 19th century. The present boundaries of Sarawak were achieved by 1906.

Northeastern Borneo, the territory that is now Sabah, was the last area to be brought under British control. In the early 1700s Brunei transferred its claims over much of the region to the sultan of Sulu, who ruled from the Sulu Archipelago (now part of the Philippines) to the east. Except in the far northeast, actual Sulu power remained limited. Occasional local resistance to Brunei or Sulu influence, as well as extensive coastal raiding and confusion of suzerainty, invited Western interest beginning in the 18th century. Despite short-lived American activity in the 1860s, British power proved most decisive. By 1846 the British had already acquired the offshore island of Labuan from Brunei. They gained a toehold in northeastern Borneo proper in 1872, when British merchant William Cowie founded an east-coast settlement at Sandakan, on lease from Sulu. Having obtained rights to much of the territory by 1881, the British launched the British North Borneo Company, which, based in Sandakan, ruled the British protectorate—as North Borneo—until 1941. The company operated the state in the interest of its shareholders but was only moderately prosperous, owing to high overhead and poor management; its 60 years of rule, however, established the economic, administrative, and political framework of contemporary Sabah.

THE IMPACT OF BRITISH RULE

The British presence in the region reflected several patterns: direct colonial rule in the Straits Settlements, relatively indirect control in some of the peninsula's east-coast sultanates, and family or corporate control in Borneo. Regardless of the political form, however, British rule brought profound changes, transforming the various states socially and economically.

The Brookes and the North Borneo Company faced prolonged resistance before they consolidated their control, while occasional local revolts punctuated British rule in Malaya as well. In Sarawak in 1857, for example, interior Chinese gold-mining communities nearly succeeded in toppling the intrusive James Brooke before being crushed, while Muslim chief Mat Salleh fought expanding British power in North Borneo from 1895 to 1900. The Brookes mounted bloody military campaigns to suppress headhunting (practiced at the time by many indigenous peoples of the interior) and to incorporate especially the Iban into their domain; similar operations were carried out in North Borneo. Those who resisted British annexation or policies were portrayed by the British authorities as treacherous, reactionary rebels; many of the same figures, however, were later hailed in Malaysia as nationalist heroes.

The British administration eventually achieved peace and security. In Malaya the Malay sultans retained their symbolic status at the apex of an aristocratic social system, although they lost some of their political authority and independence. British officials believed that the rural Malay farmers needed to be protected from economic and cultural change and that traditional class divisions should be maintained. Hence, most economic development was left to Chinese and Indian immigrants, as long as it served long-term colonial interests. The Malay elite enjoyed a place in the new colonial order as civil servants.

Many Malayan and Bornean villagers, however, were affected by colonial taxes and consequently were forced to shift from subsistence to cash-crop farming; their economic well-being became subject to fluctuations in world commodity prices. Much economic growth occurred; British policies promoted the planting of pepper, gambier (a plant producing a resin used for tanning and dyeing), tobacco, oil palm, and especially rubber, which along with tin became the region's major exports. Malaya and British North Borneo developed extractive, plantation-based economies oriented toward the resource and market needs of the industrializing West.

This 1843 painting depicts an English ship off the coast of Sarawak.

British authorities in Malaya devoted much effort to constructing a transportation infrastructure in which railways and road networks linked the tin fields to the coast; port facilities also were improved to facilitate resource exports. These developments stimulated growth in the tin and rubber industries to meet world demand. The tin industry remained chiefly in immigrant Chinese hands through the 19th century, but more highly capitalized, technologically sophisticated British firms took over much of the tin production and export by World War II. The rubber tree was first introduced from Brazil in the 1870s, but rubber did not supersede the earlier coffee and gambier plantings until near the end of the century. By the early 20th century thousands of acres of forest had been cleared for rubber growing, much of it on plantations but some on smallholdings. Malaya became the world's greatest exporter of natural rubber, with rubber and tin providing the bulk of colonial tax revenues.

The British also improved public health facilities, which reduced the incidence of various tropical diseases, and they facilitated the establishment of government Malay schools and Christian mission (mostly English-language) schools; the Chinese generally had to develop their own schools. These separate school systems helped perpetuate the pluralistic

society. Some Chinese, Malays, and Indians benefited from British economic policies; others enjoyed
no improvement or experienced a drop in their
standard of living. Government-sanctioned opium
and alcohol use provided a major source of revenue
in some areas.

Between 1800 and 1941 several million Chinese entered Malaya (especially the west-coast
states), Sarawak, and British North Borneo to work
as labourers, miners, planters, and merchants. The
Chinese eventually became part of a prosperous,
urban middle class that controlled retail trade. South
Indian Tamils were imported as the workforce on
Malayan rubber estates. At the turn of the 19th century Malays accounted for the vast majority of Malaya's residents, but the influx of immigrants over
the subsequent decades significantly eroded that
majority. A compartmentalized society developed
on the peninsula, and colonial authorities skillfully
utilized "divide and rule" tactics to maintain their
control. With most Malays in villages, Chinese in
towns, and Indians on plantations, the various ethnic
groups basically lived in their own neighbourhoods,
followed different occupations, practiced their own
religions, spoke their own languages, operated their
own schools, and, later, formed their own political

organizations. By the 1930s ethnically oriented nationalist currents began to stir in Malaya, Singapore, and Sarawak. Malay groups either pursued Islamic revitalization and reform or debated the future of the Malays in a plural society, while Chinese organizations framed their activities around political trends in China.

The Borneo states experienced many of the same changes. Sir Charles Brooke, second raja of Sarawak, passed the state on to his son, Charles Vyner de Windt Brooke, in 1917. Vyner Brooke reigned until 1946, furthering the pattern of personal rule established by his father and by his great-uncle, Sir James Brooke. Economic incentives attracted Chinese immigrants, and by 1939 the Chinese accounted for about one-fourth of the state's population. Similar to Malaya, Sarawak became ethnically, occupationally, and socially segmented, with most Malays in government or fishing, most Chinese in trade, labour, or cash-crop farming, and most Iban in the police force or shifting cultivation. Gambier and pepper were planted, with Sarawak emerging as the major world supplier of the latter crop. Later, rubber became dominant, and a petroleum industry developed. Most cash-crop agriculture remained in smallholdings rather than in the plantations that were characteristic elsewhere. Christian missionary activity and church, Chinese, and Malay schools also generated sociocultural change. In the 1930s ethnic consciousness rose among both the Chinese and the Malay communities as Vyner Brooke's personal rule began to erode.

The North Borneo Company operated differently from the Brookes in that it concentrated on developing an extractive economy for the benefit of its shareholders, based mostly on Western-owned tobacco and rubber estates and forest exploitation. Like the Brookes, however, the company created a single state out of many local societies and tolerated little open political activity. Christian missions facilitated change among non-Muslims. Significantly, immigrant Chinese and Indonesians also diversified the population through their employment as plantation workers.

POLITICAL TRANSFORMATION

The occupation of Malaya and Borneo by Japan (1942–45) during World War II generated tremendous changes in those territories. Their economies were disrupted, and communal tensions were exacerbated because Malays and Chinese reacted differently to Japanese control. The Japanese desperately needed access to the natural resources of Southeast

Asia; they invaded Malaya in December 1941, having neutralized American military power in Hawaii through the Pearl Harbor attack and in the Philippines through attacks on Manila. Shortly thereafter, the Japanese controlled the peninsula, Singapore, and Borneo. Pro-communist, predominantly Chinese guerrillas waged resistance in Malaya, and a brief Chinese-led revolt also erupted in North Borneo. In many places increasing politicization and conflict within and among ethnic groups developed as a result of economic hardship and selective repression; in northern Borneo the rule of the Brookes and of the North Borneo Company was permanently undermined, while in Malaya the Chinese and Malays also realized that British domination was not everlasting. Nonetheless, most people welcomed the Japanese defeat in 1945.

After the end of the war, Sarawak and North Borneo, both of which had been British protectorates until the Japanese occupation, became British crown colonies. Sarawak, however, faced a turbulent political situation. Many Malays opposed the termination of Brooke rule and Sarawak's cession to Britain, and the resulting sociopolitical divisions persisted for years. With the establishment of the British North Borneo colony, the capital was moved from Sandakan to Jesselton (now Kota Kinabalu). Some local self-government was introduced in Malaya. The major catalyst of political organization, however, was a British proposal to form a single Malayan Union, incorporating all the Malayan territories except Singapore, that would diminish state autonomy and accord equal political and citizenship rights to non-Malays. A tremendous upsurge of Malay political feeling against this plan, led by Dato' Onn bin Jaafar, resulted in the creation in 1946 of the United Malays National Organization (UMNO) as a vehicle for Malay nationalism and political assertiveness. Strikes, demonstrations, and boycotts doomed the proposed Malayan Union, and the British began to negotiate with UMNO about the Malayan future.

The negotiations resulted in the creation in 1948 of the Federation of Malaya, which unified the territories but provided special guarantees of Malay rights, including the position of the sultans. These developments alarmed the more radical and impoverished sectors of the Chinese community. In 1948 the Communist Party of Malaya—a mostly Chinese movement formed in 1930 that had provided the backbone of the anti-Japanese resistance—went into the jungles and began a guerrilla insurgency to defeat the colonial government, sparking a 12-year period of unrest known as the Malayan Emergency. The communists waged a violent and ultimately futile struggle supported by only a small segment of the Chinese community. The British took measures to suppress the insurgency by military means, which included a strategy that forcibly moved many rural Chinese into tightly controlled New Villages located near or along the roadsides. Although this policy isolated villagers from guerrillas, it also increased the government's unpopularity. The British finally achieved success when, under the leadership of British high commissioner Sir Gerald Templer, they actively began to address political and economic grievances as well as the insurgency, which further isolated the rebels.

Promising independence, British officials commenced negotiations with the various ethnic leaders, including those of UMNO and the Malayan Chinese Association (MCA), formed in 1949 by wealthy Chinese businessmen. A coalition consisting of UMNO (led by the aristocratic moderate Tunku Abdul Rahman), MCA, and the Malayan Indian Congress contested the national legislative elections held in 1955 and won all but one seat. This established a permanent political pattern of a ruling coalition—known first as the Alliance Party and later as the National

Front (Barisan Nasional; BN)—that united ethnically based, mostly elite-led parties of moderate to conservative political leanings, with UMNO as the major force.

On Aug. 31, 1957, the Federation of Malaya achieved independence under an Alliance government headed by Tunku Abdul Rahman as prime minister. Singapore, with its predominantly Chinese population, remained outside the federation as a British crown colony. The arrangement tended to favour the Malays politically, with UMNO leaders holding most federal and state offices and the kingship rotating among the various Malay sultans, but the Chinese were granted liberal citizenship rights and maintained strong economic power. Kuala Lumpur became the federal capital.

New currents also were emerging in Borneo. Colonial rule succeeded in rebuilding and expanding the economies of the two colonies, with rubber and timber providing the basis for postwar economic growth. Health and education facilities slowly reached beyond the towns. Political consciousness began to spread as elections were held for local councils. During the 1950s the Kadazan community, stimulated particularly by the development of radio broadcasting and newspapers, became involved in North Borneo politics, while Chinese and Malay leaders formed Sarawak's first political parties—some espousing multiethnic identities—in expectation of independence. Political activity accelerated with the mooting in 1961 of the proposal by Malayan and British officials for a federated state that would include Malaya, Sarawak, North Borneo, Brunei, and Singapore. New parties formed in North Borneo representing the Kadazan, Chinese, and various Muslim communities. Elections were held in North Borneo and in Sarawak, with most of the parties in both colonies accepting independence through merging with the new federation, called Malaysia; the inclination to join Malaysia increased after the Philippines claimed North Borneo, based on former Sulu suzerainty.

British leaders proposed a Malaysian federation as a way of terminating their now burdensome colonial rule over Singapore, Sarawak, and North Borneo, even though those states were historically and ethnically distinct from Malaya and from each other. It was in many ways to be a marriage of convenience. Malaya was closely linked economically with bustling Singapore, and the Malays felt a kinship to the various Muslim groups in Borneo. Tunku Abdul Rahman believed the federation could defuse potential leftist Chinese activity while balancing the Chinese majority in Singapore with the non-Chinese majorities of the Borneo states. Malaya already contained a Chinese minority of nearly 40 percent, with Malays barely in the majority there. Hence, on Sept. 16, 1963, the Federation of Malaysia was formed, with North Borneo—renamed Sabah—and Sarawak constituting East Malaysia. Brunei, which had been invited to join, chose to remain a British protectorate and later became independent as a small, oil-rich Malay sultanate.

MYANMAR

Following the Third Anglo-Burmese War, Myanmar became a British colony known as Burma. The loss of independence was painful enough; worse still were the British decisions to eliminate the monarchy—in the process sending Thibaw into exile—and to detach the government from religious affairs, thus depriving the sangha (monkhood) of its traditional status and official patronage. Moreover, the British eliminated the office of the patriarch of the Buddhist clergy. The demise of the monarchy and the monkhood, the twin pillars of the society of Myanmar, was perhaps the most devastating aspect of the colonial period.

THE ANGLO-BURMESE WARS

Myanmar came face to face with British power in India when it conquered Rakhine and occupied the princely state of Assam to the northwest of Manipur. The result was the First Anglo-Burmese War (1824–26), in which the Siamese fought on the British side. Myanmar eventually had to sue for peace and relinquish Assam, Manipur, Rakhine, and Tenasserim.

The Second Anglo-Burmese War (1852) was provoked by the British, who wanted access to the teak forests in and around Bago and also wanted to secure the gap in their coastline stretching from Calcutta (Kolkata) to Singapore; it resulted in the British annexation of Bago province, which they renamed Lower Burma. As the British became increasingly interested in the legendary trade with China through its back door—as well as in the teak, oil, and rubies of northern Myanmar—they waited for a suitable pretext to attack. In 1885 Britain declared war on Myanmar for the third and final time. To meet the

(CONTINUED ON PAGE 219)

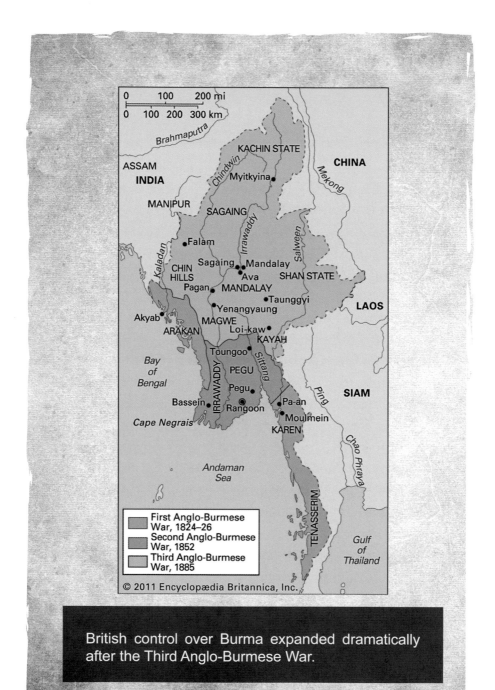

British control over Burma expanded dramatically after the Third Anglo-Burmese War.

(CONTINUED FROM PAGE 217)

criticism of this action that arose in Parliament, the British government gave the excuses that the last independent king of Myanmar, Thibaw (ruled 1878–85), was a tyrant and that he was conspiring to give France greater influence over the country. Neither of these charges seems to have had much foundation.

The third of the Anglo-Burmese Wars lasted less than two weeks during November 1885, with the British taking Mandalay, which had become the capital of northern Myanmar in 1857, with remarkable alacrity. The hopelessly outmatched royal troops surrendered quickly, although armed resistance continued for several years. The people of Myanmar believed that the British aim was merely to replace King Thibaw with a prince who had been sheltered and groomed in India for the throne. This did not come to pass, however, as the British finally decided not only to annex all of northern Myanmar (which they called Upper Burma) as a colony but also to make the whole country a province of India (effective Jan. 1, 1886). Rangoon (now Yangon) became the capital of the province, after having been the capital of British Lower Burma.

THE INITIAL IMPACT OF COLONIALISM

Many refused to accept the British victory and resorted to guerrilla warfare against the British army of occupation. The guerrillas were led mainly by former officers of the disbanded royal army, former officials (including village headmen), and royal princes, and they considered themselves to be royal soldiers still fighting the Third Anglo-Burmese War. To the British, however, the war had ended legally with the annexation of the kingdom; those opposing them, therefore, were considered rebels and bandits. For the next five years the British military officers acted as both judge and jury in dealing with captured guerrillas. Villagers who aided the rebels also were sternly punished. British troops carried out mass executions and committed other atrocities.

As the guerrillas fought on, the British adopted a "strategic hamlet" strategy, whereby villages were burned and families who had supplied villages with their headmen were uprooted from their homes and sent away to Lower Burma (which had been under British control since the Second Anglo-Burmese War). Strangers loyal to the colonial government were appointed as headmen for the new villages established by the British. The guerrillas resorted to desperate measures against the new village officials. By 1890, however, with more than 30,000 British and Indian troops engaged in the campaign, the military part of the struggle was over.

THE RELIGIOUS DILEMMA

The colonial period was one of relative civil order, but it also was one of great social disintegration. Chief among the reasons for this was the British-imposed separation of the sangha and the state. The British did not wish to touch the issue of religion—given their experience in India that had led to the Indian Mutiny beginning in 1857—and thus they were unwilling to patronize Burmese Buddhism as the monarchy had done.

Under the monarchy, the monkhood and the state had shared a symbiotic relationship. Royal patronage of Burmese Buddhism had included both financial and moral support, which had extended legitimacy and authority to the religious institution. The king had had the right to appoint the patriarch, who exercised supervision and discipline among the ranks of the clergy. In addition,

Burmese children before a statue of the Buddha in the late 19th century. Buddhism remains the predominant religion in modern-day Myanmar.

the king had been given the right to attach two royal officials to the patriarch: a commissioner of ecclesiastical lands and an ecclesiastical censor. The duty of the land commissioner had been to see that ecclesiastical lands were exempted from payment of taxes, at the same time ensuring that false and illegal endowments did not escape taxation. The duty of the censor had been to maintain a register of monks, which had given the king indirect control over the clergy. The power to defrock a wayward monk had rested largely with the patriarch, but the same result could be achieved if the king declared the monk to be impure, which was one of the king's prerogatives. This arrangement was designed to prevent the abuse of the exemptions granted to the clergy.

The British refusal to heed a plea by the clergy and religious elders to continue the traditional relationship between the monkhood and the state resulted in the decline of the sangha and its ability to instill discipline in the clergy. This in turn lowered the prestige of the clergy and contributed to the rise of secular education and of a new class of teachers, depriving the sangha of one of its primary roles. Added to this, the colonial government of India founded secular schools teaching in both English and Burmese and encouraged foreign Christian missions to found schools by offering them financial assistance. Many mission schools were founded; parents were compelled to send their children to these schools, as there were no realistic alternatives. The teachers were missionaries, and the lessons they gave were marked by repeated criticism of Buddhism and its culture. In the government schools the first teachers, British and Indian, were mere civil servants, unable and unwilling to continue the older traditions.

THE COLONIAL ECONOMY

Under the monarchy, the economy of Myanmar had been one of redistribution, a concept embedded in local society, religion, and politics. Prices of the most important commodities were set by the state, and in general the mechanism of supply and demand was relatively unimportant. Agrarian self-sufficiency was vital, while trade was only of secondary importance. The British impact on this system proved disastrous, as Burma's economy became part of the vast export-oriented enterprise of western colonialism. With the British—rather than the people of Burma—as the intended beneficiaries of the new economy, the traditional Burmese economic system collapsed.

The British dream of a golden road to China through Burma could not be realized, but the opening of the Suez Canal in 1869 created a much higher international demand for Burma's rice than had previously existed. The Irrawaddy delta was swiftly cleared of its mangrove forests and in a matter of decades became covered with rice fields. The area of productive rice fields in Lower Burma rose from approximately 60,000 acres (24,000 hectares) to nearly 10,000,000 acres (4,000,000 hectares) between the mid-19th century and the outbreak of World War II, while the price of rice increased rapidly and continuously until the Great Depression of the 1930s. This tremendous increase in production created a significant shift in population from the northern heartland to the delta, shifting as well the basis of wealth and power.

In order to prepare the land for cultivation, however, the farmers had to borrow capital from Indian moneylenders from Madras (Chennai) at exorbitant interest rates. The British banks would not grant mortgage loans on rice land, and the British government had no policy for establishing land-mortgage banks or for making agricultural loans. Prevailing prices were high in the international market, but the local price was kept down by a handful of British firms that controlled wholesale trade and by Indian and Chinese merchants who controlled retail trade. With land values and rice prices soaring, the Indian moneylenders foreclosed mortgages at the earliest opportunity, especially when the Great Depression disrupted trade.

The dispossessed farmers could not find employment even on their lost lands because, with their higher standard of living, they could not compete with the thousands of Indian labourers who went to Burma. Burmese villagers, unemployed and lost in a disintegrating society, sometimes took to petty theft and robbery and were soon characterized by the British as lazy and undisciplined. The level of dysfunction in Burmese society was revealed by the dramatic rise in homicides.

Thus, although the Burmese economy and transportation infrastructure developed rapidly from 1890 to 1900, the majority of Burmese people did not benefit from it. A railway had been built through the entire valley of the Irrawaddy, and hundreds of steamboats plied the length of the river, but the railway and the boats belonged to British companies. Roads had been built by the government, but they were meant for the swift transport of troops. A British company worked the ruby mines until they became nearly exhausted. The extraction of petroleum and timber was monopolized by two British firms. The balance of trade was always in favour of Burma, but that meant little to Burmese people or society.

THE EMERGENCE OF NATIONALISM

Those Burmese who attended the new schools established by the colonial government or by missionaries managed to gain admission to the clerical grades of government service, but even in those lower grades they encountered competition from Indians. Because science courses were not available, the professions of engineering and medicine were closed to the Burmese. Those who advanced to the government liberal arts college at Rangoon (Yangon) entered the middle grades of the civil service, while a few went on to London to study law. When these young barristers returned to Burma, they were looked upon by the people as their new leaders. Their sojourn in the liberal atmosphere of London had convinced these new leaders that some measure of political independence could be regained by negotiation.

The new leaders first turned their attention to the national religion, culture, and education. In 1906 they founded the Young Men's Buddhist Association (YMBA) and through it began establishing a number of schools supported by private donations and government grants-in-aid (the YMBA was not antigovernment). Three years later the British, attempting to pacify the Indian National Congress (a broadly based and increasingly nationalist political party in India), introduced some constitutional reforms in India. Only a few minor changes were made in the Burmese constitution, but these confirmed the young leaders' faith in British liberalism. In 1920, however, when it was learned that Burma would be excluded from new reforms introduced in India, the barristers led the people in a countrywide protest, which involved a boycott of British goods.

Also in 1920 Rangoon College was raised to the status of a full university by the University Act. However, because the accompanying changes in the school's administration and curriculum were viewed as elitist and exclusionary of the Burmese population, its students went on strike. Younger schoolchildren followed suit, and the general public and the Buddhist clergy gave full support to the movement. The strikers camped in the courtyards of monasteries, reviving memories of days when education was the concern of the monks. The University Act eventually was amended and the strike settled, but many strikers initially refused to go back to mission and government schools. The YMBA schools, now calling themselves "national" schools, opened their doors to the strikers.

Constitutional reforms were finally granted in 1923, but the delay had split the leaders, some of whom, like the masses, were beginning to doubt whether political freedom could be attained by peaceful protest. At the University of Rangoon itself, students began to resent their British professors. A radical student group began organizing protests, which came to be known as the Thakin movement. The name for this movement was purposely ironic: the Burmese word *thakin* ("master") was the term that the Burmese were required to use when addressing the British.

Late in 1930 Burmese peasants, under the leadership of Saya San, rose in rebellion. Armed only with swords and sticks, they resisted British and Indian troops for two years. The young Thakins, though not involved in the rebellion, won the trust of the villagers and emerged as leaders in place of the British-educated Burmese elite. In 1936 university students again went on strike, and two of their leaders, Thakin Nu (later called U Nu) and Aung San, joined the Thakin movement. In 1937 the British government separated Burma from India and granted it its own constitution, independent of that of India; the masses interpreted this as proof that the British planned to exclude Burma from the next phase of Indian reform.

WORLD WAR II AND AFTER

When World War II erupted in Europe in 1939, the Burmese leaders wanted to bargain with the government before giving their support to the British. A warrant was issued for the arrest of Aung San, but he escaped to China, where he attempted to solicit support from radical groups. Assistance came instead from the Japanese government. Aung San returned to Burma in secret, recruited 29 young men, and took them to Japan, where these "Thirty Comrades" (including Ne Win, who later became head of state) received military training. The Japanese promised independence for Burma; hence, when Japanese troops reached Bangkok (Thailand) in December 1941, Aung San announced the formation of the Burma Independence Army (BIA). The Japanese advanced into Burma and by the end of 1942 had occupied the country. They subsequently disbanded the BIA and formed a smaller Burma Defense Army, with Aung San still as commander. Meanwhile, Thailand was given territory in the Shan states for its support of Japan's wartime efforts; those lands were returned to Burma in the postwar period, however.

Ba Maw, the first prime minister under the 1937 constitution and later the leader of the opposition, was appointed head of state by the Japanese, with a cabinet including Aung San and Thakin Nu. In 1943, when the tide of battle started to turn against them, the Japanese declared Burma a fully sovereign state. The Burmese government, however, was still a mere facade, with the Japanese army ruling. Meanwhile, Aung San had contacted Lord Louis Mountbatten, the Allied commander in Southeast Asia, as early as October 1943 to offer his cooperation, and in March 1945 Aung San and his army—renamed the Burma National Army (BNA)—joined the British side.

During the war Aung San and the Thakins formed a coalition of political parties called the Anti-Fascist

Organization—renamed the Anti-Fascist People's Freedom League (AFPFL) after the war—which had wide popular support. After the defeat of the Japanese in Burma in May 1945, the British military administration and members of the prewar government who had returned from exile demanded that Aung San be tried as a traitor. Mountbatten, however, recognized the extent of Aung San's hold on the BNA and on the general populace, and he hastily sent the more conciliatory Sir Hubert Rance to head the administration. Rance regained for the British the trust of Aung San and the general public. When the war ended, the military administration was withdrawn, and Rance was replaced by the former civilian governor, who formed a cabinet consisting of older and more conservative politicians. The new administration arrested Aung San and charged him with treason. Surprised and angered, the Burmese people prepared for rebellion, but the British government in London wisely reinstated Rance, who had proven himself a sensitive and successful administrator in Burma, as governor.

Rance formed a new cabinet, including Aung San, and discussions for a peaceful transfer of power began. These were concluded in London in January 1947, when the British agreed to Burma's independence. By June the Burmese had decided to leave the British Commonwealth of Nations.

The communist and conservative wings of the AFPFL were dissatisfied with the agreement. The communists broke away and went underground, and the conservatives went into opposition. In July Aung San and most members of his cabinet were assassinated by gunmen sent by U Saw, a former prime minister and now a conservative. Rance asked Thakin Nu to form a new cabinet. A new constitution was written, and on Jan. 4, 1948, Burma became a sovereign, independent republic.

INDEPENDENCE

With its economy shattered and its towns and villages destroyed during the war, Burma needed peace. A foreign policy of neutrality was decided upon, but, because of internal strife, no peace resulted. The communists were the first insurgents, followed by some of Aung San's veterans and then the Karen, the only ethnic minority on the plains. The other minorities—Chin, Kachin, and Shan—who had been ruled separately by the British but who had enthusiastically joined the union, stood firm in support of the government.

At the United Nations, Burma endeavoured to show impartiality. It was one of the first countries to recognize Israel, as well as the People's Republic of

China. Meanwhile, a division of Chinese Nationalist troops occupied parts of the Shan Plateau after their defeat by the Chinese communists in 1949. Because of the general support given to Nationalist China (Taiwan) by the United States, Burma stopped accepting U.S. aid and rejected all other foreign aid.

By 1958 Burma was well on the road to internal peace and economic recovery, but the ruling AFPFL had become divided by personal quarrels between U Nu (formerly called Thakin Nu) and his closest associates. Amid rumours of a military takeover, U Nu invited the army chief of staff, Ne Win—who had been a Thakin, one of the Thirty Comrades, and Aung San's second in command—to assume the premiership. This move sometimes has been called a "constitutional coup." Ne Win established internal security, stabilized the military situation, and prepared the country for general elections, which took place in February 1960. U Nu was returned to office with an absolute majority.

CHAPTER EIGHT

VIETNAM

• •

Vietnam has a long history of affiliating with a dominant civilization and adapting that civilization's ideas, institutions, and technology to Vietnamese purposes. This pattern of affiliating and adapting was already evident in Vietnam's historical relations with China, and it reappeared as descendants of mandarins responded to the challenge of the West by rejecting tradition and becoming communists to combat colonialism. The pattern was evident again as it animated 20th-century artistic movements that employed Western forms to promote social renovation.

In 1516 Portuguese adventurers arriving by sea inaugurated the era of Western penetration of Vietnam. They were followed in 1527 by Dominican missionaries, and eight years later a Portuguese port and trading centre were established at Faifo (modern Hoi An), south of present-day Da Nang. More Portuguese missionaries arrived later in the 16th century, and they were followed by other Europeans. The best-known of these was the French Jesuit missionary Alexandre de Rhodes, who completed a transcription of the Vietnamese language into Roman script that later was adopted by modern Vietnamese as their official writing system, Quoc-ngu ("national language").

By the end of the 17th century, however, the two rival Vietnamese domains (under the Nguyen family in the south, and the Trinh family in the north) had lost interest in maintaining relations with European countries; the only window left open to the West was at Faifo, where the Portuguese retained a trading mission. For decades the French had tried without success to retain some influence in the area. Only at the end of the 18th century was a missionary named Pigneau de Béhaine able to restore a French presence by assisting Nguyen Anh in wresting control of Dai Viet from the Tay Sons.

Upon becoming emperor, however, Nguyen Anh (now Gia Long) did not favour Christianity. Under his strongly anti-Western successor, Minh Mang (ruled 1820–41), all French advisers were dismissed, while seven French missionaries and an unknown number of Vietnamese Christians were executed. After 1840 French Roman Catholic interests openly demanded military intervention to prevent the persecution of missionaries. In 1847 the French took reprisals against Vietnam for expelling additional missionaries, but 10 years passed before Paris prepared a military expedition against Vietnam.

THE CONQUEST OF VIETNAM BY FRANCE

The decision to invade Vietnam was made by Napoleon III in July 1857. It was the result not only of missionary propaganda but also, after 1850, of the upsurge of French capitalism, which generated the need for overseas markets and the desire for a larger French share of the Asian territories conquered by the West. The naval commander in East Asia, Rigault de Genouilly, long an advocate of French military action against Vietnam, was ordered to attack the harbour and city of Tourane (Da Nang) and to turn it into a French military base. Genouilly arrived at Tourane in August 1858 with 14 vessels and 2,500 men; the French stormed the harbour defenses on September 1 and occupied the town a day later. Genouilly soon recognized, however, that he could make no further progress around Tourane and decided to attack Saigon. Leaving a small garrison behind to hold Tourane, he sailed southward in February 1859 and seized Saigon two weeks later.

Vietnamese resistance prevented the French from advancing beyond Saigon, and it took French troops, under new command, until 1861 to occupy the three adjacent provinces. The Vietnamese, unable to mount effective resistance to the invaders and their advanced weapons, concluded a peace treaty in June 1862, which ceded the conquered territories to France. Five years later additional territories in the south were placed under French rule. The entire colony was named Cochinchina.

It had taken the French slightly more than eight years to make themselves masters of Cochinchina (a protectorate already had been imposed on Cambodia in 1863). It took them 16 more years to extend their control over the rest of the country. They made a first attempt to enter the Red River delta in 1873, after a French naval officer and explorer named Francis Garnier had shown, in a hazardous expedition, that the Mekong River could not serve as a trade route into southwestern China. Garnier had some support from the French governor of Cochinchina, but when he was killed in a battle with Chinese pirates near Hanoi, the attempt to conquer the north collapsed.

Within a decade, France had returned to the challenge. In April 1882, with the blessing of Paris, the administration at Saigon sent a force of 250 men to Hanoi under Capt. Henri Rivière. When Rivière was killed in a skirmish, Paris moved to impose its rule by force over the entire Red River delta. In August 1883 the Vietnamese court signed a treaty that turned northern Vietnam (named Tonkin by the French) and central Vietnam (named Annam, based on an early Chinese name for the region) into French protectorates. Ten years later the French annexed Laos and added it to the so-called Indochinese Union, which the French created in 1887. The union consisted of the colony of Cochinchina and the four protectorates of Annam, Tonkin, Cambodia, and Laos.

COLONIAL VIETNAM

The French now moved to impose a Western-style administration on their colonial territories and to open them to economic exploitation. Under Gov.-Gen. Paul Doumer, who arrived in 1897, French rule was imposed directly at all levels of administration, leaving the Vietnamese bureaucracy without any real power. Even Vietnamese emperors were deposed at will and replaced by others willing to serve the French. All important positions within the bureaucracy were staffed with officials imported from France; even in the 1930s, after several periods of reforms and concessions to local nationalist sentiment, Vietnamese officials were employed only in minor positions and

Gov.-Gen. Albert Sarraut (*left*) sits with Emperor Khai Dinh in 1918.

at very low salaries, and the country was still administered along the lines laid down by Doumer.

Doumer's economic and social policies also determined, for the entire period of French rule, the development of French Indochina, as the colony became known in the 20th century. The railroads, highways, harbours, bridges, canals, and other public works built by the French were almost all started under Doumer, whose aim was a rapid and systematic exploitation of Indochina's potential wealth for the benefit of France; Vietnam was to become a source of raw materials and a market for tariff-protected goods produced by French industries. The exploitation of natural resources for direct export was the chief purpose of all French investments, with rice, coal, rare minerals, and later also rubber as the main products.

Doumer and his successors up to the eve of World War II were not interested in promoting industry there, the development of which was limited to the production of goods for immediate local consumption. Among these enterprises—located chiefly in Saigon, Hanoi, and Haiphong (the outport for Hanoi)—were breweries, distilleries, small sugar refineries, rice and paper mills, and glass and cement factories. The greatest industrial establishment was a textile factory at Nam Dinh, which employed more than 5,000 workers. The total number of workers employed by all industries and mines in Vietnam was some 100,000 in 1930. Because the aim of all investments was not the systematic economic development of the colony but the attainment of immediate high returns for investors, only a small fraction of the profits was reinvested.

Whatever economic progress Vietnam made under the French after 1900 benefited only the French and the small class of wealthy Vietnamese created by the colonial regime. The masses of the Vietnamese people were deprived of such benefits by the social policies inaugurated by Doumer and maintained even by his more liberal successors, such as Paul Beau (1902–07), Albert Sarraut (1911–14 and 1917–19), and Alexandre Varenne (1925–28).

Apologists for the colonial regime claimed that French rule led to vast improvements in medical care, education, transport, and communications. The statistics kept by the French, however, appear to cast doubt on such assertions. In 1939, for example, no more than 15 percent of all school-age children received any kind of schooling, and about 80 percent of the population was illiterate, in contrast to precolonial times when the majority of the people possessed some degree of literacy. With its more than 20 million inhabitants in 1939, Vietnam had but one university, with fewer than 700 students. Only a

AGRICULTURE IN FRENCH INDOCHINA

Through the construction of irrigation works, chiefly in the Mekong delta, the area of land devoted to rice cultivation quadrupled between 1880 and 1930. During the same period, however, the individual peasant's rice consumption decreased without the substitution of other foods. The new lands were not distributed among the landless and the peasants but were sold to the highest bidder or given away at nominal prices to Vietnamese collaborators and French speculators. These policies created a new class of Vietnamese landlords and a class of landless tenants who worked the fields of the landlords for rents of up to 60 percent of the crop, which was sold by the landlords at the Saigon export market. The mounting export figures for rice resulted not only from the increase in cultivable land but also from the growing exploitation of the peasantry.

The peasants who owned their land were rarely better off than the landless tenants. The peasants' share of the price of rice sold at the Saigon export market was less than 25 percent. Peasants continually lost their land to the large owners because they were unable to repay loans given them by the landlords and other money-lenders at exorbitant interest rates. As a result, the large landowners of Cochinchina (less than 3 percent of the total number of landowners) owned 45 percent of the land, while the small peasants (who accounted for about 70 percent of the owners) owned only about 15 percent of the land. The number of landless families in Vietnam before World War II was estimated at half of the population.

The peasants' share of the crop—after the landlords, the moneylenders, and the middlemen (mostly Chinese) between producer and exporter had taken their share—was reduced even more drastically by the direct and indirect taxes the French had imposed to finance their ambitious program of public works. Other ways of making the Vietnamese pay for the projects undertaken for the benefit of the French were the recruitment of forced labour for public works and the absence of any protection against exploitation in the mines and rubber plantations, although the scan-dalous working conditions, the low salaries, and the lack of medical care were frequently attacked in the French Chamber of Deputies in Paris. The mild social legislation decreed in the late 1920s was never adequately enforced.

small number of Vietnamese children were admitted to the lycées (secondary schools) for the children of the French. Medical care was well organized for the French in the cities, but in 1939 there were only 2 physicians for every 100,000 Vietnamese, compared with 76 per 100,000 in Japan and 25 per 100,000 in the Philippines.

Two other aspects of French colonial policy are significant when considering the attitude of the Vietnamese people, especially their educated minority, toward the colonial regime: one was the absence of any kind of civil liberties for the native population, and the other was the exclusion of the Vietnamese from the modern sector of the economy, especially industry and trade. Not only were rubber plantations, mines, and industrial enterprises in foreign hands—French, where the business was substantial, and Chinese at the lower levels—but all other business was as well, from local trade to the great export-import houses. The social consequence of this policy was that, apart from the landlords, no property-owning indigenous middle class developed in colonial Vietnam. Thus, capitalism appeared to the Vietnamese to be a part of foreign rule; this view, together with the lack of any Vietnamese participation in government, profoundly influenced the nature and orientation of the national resistance movements.

MOVEMENTS OF NATIONAL LIBERATION

The anticolonial movement in Vietnam can be said to have started with the establishment of French rule. Many local officials of Cochinchina refused to collaborate with the French. Some led guerrilla groups, composed of the remnants of the defeated armies, in attacks on French outposts. A much broader resistance movement developed in Annam in 1885, led by the great scholar Phan Dinh Phung, whose rebellion collapsed only after his death in 1895.

The main characteristic of the national movement during this first phase of resistance, however, was its political orientation toward the past. Filled with ideas of precolonial Vietnam, its leaders wanted to be rid of the French in order to reestablish the old imperial order. Because this aspiration had little meaning for the generation that came to maturity after 1900, this first stage of anticolonial resistance did not survive the death of its leader.

A new national movement arose in the early 20th century. Its most prominent spokesman was Phan Boi Chau, with whose rise the old traditionalist opposition gave way to a modern nationalist leadership that rejected French rule but not Western ideas, science, and technology. In 1905 Chau went to Japan. His plan, mildly encouraged by some Japanese states-men, was to free Vietnam with Japanese help. Chau smuggled hundreds of young Vietnamese into Ja-pan, where they studied the sciences and underwent training for clandestine organization, political propa-ganda, and terrorist action. Inspired by Chau's writ-ings, nationalist intellectuals in Hanoi opened the Free School of Tonkin in 1907, which soon became a centre of anti-French agitation and consequently was suppressed after a few months. Also, under the inspiration and guidance of Chau's followers, mass demonstrations demanding a reduction of high taxes took place in many cities in 1908. Hundreds of dem-onstrators and suspected organizers were arrested—some were condemned to death, while others were sent to Con Son (Poulo Condore) Island in the South China Sea, which the French turned into a penal camp for Vietnamese nationalists.

Phan Boi Chau went to China in 1910, where a revolution had broken out against the Qing (Man-chu) dynasty. There he set up a republican govern-ment-in-exile to attract the support of nationalist groups. After the French arranged his arrest and im-prisonment in China (1914–17), however, his move-ment began to decline. In 1925 Chau was seized by French agents in Shanghai and brought back to Vietnam for trial; he died under house arrest in 1940.

After World War I the movement for national liberation intensified. A number of prominent intellectuals sought to achieve reforms by obtaining political concessions from the colonial regime through collaboration with the French. The failure of such reformist efforts led to a revival of clandestine and revolutionary groups, especially in Annam and Tonkin; among these was the Vietnamese Nationalist Party (Viet Nam Quoc Dan Dang, founded in 1927 and usually referred to as the VNQDD). The VNQDD preached terrorist action and penetrated the garrisons of indigenous troops with a plan to oust the French in a military uprising. On the night of Feb. 9–10, 1930, the troops of one garrison in Tonkin killed their French officers, but they were overwhelmed a day later and summarily executed. A wave of repression followed that took hundreds of lives and sent thousands to prison camps. The VNQDD was virtually destroyed, and for the next 15 years it existed mainly as a group of exiles in China supported by the Chinese Nationalist Party (Kuomintang).

The year 1930 was important in the history of Vietnam for yet another reason. Five years earlier, a new figure, destined to become the most prominent leader in the national movement, had appeared on the scene as an expatriate revolutionary in South China. He was Nguyen Ai Quoc, better known by his later pseudonym of Ho Chi Minh. In June 1925 Ho Chi Minh had founded the Revolutionary Youth League of Vietnam, the predecessor of the Indochinese Communist Party.

Ho Chi Minh had left Vietnam as a young seaman in 1911 and traveled widely before settling in Paris in 1917. He joined the Communist Party of France in 1920 and later spent several years in Moscow and China in the service of the international communist movement. After making his Revolutionary Youth League the most influential of all clandestine resistance groups, he succeeded in early 1930 in forming the Vietnamese Communist Party—from late 1930 called the Indochinese Communist Party—from a number of competing communist organizations. In May of that year the communists exploited conditions of

Ho Chi Minh, seen here in 1920, led the Vietnamese nationalist movement for nearly three decades.

near starvation over large areas of central Vietnam by staging a broad peasant uprising, during which numerous Vietnamese officials and many landlords were killed, and "Soviet" administrations were set up in several provinces of Annam. It took the French until the spring of 1931 to suppress this movement and, in an unparalleled wave of terror, to reestablish control.

Unlike the dispersed and disoriented leadership of the VNQDD and some smaller nationalist groups, the Indochinese Communist Party recovered quickly from the setback of 1931, relying on cadres trained in the Soviet Union and China. After 1936, when the French extended some political freedoms to the colonies, the party skillfully exploited all opportunities for the creation of legal front organizations, through which it extended its influence among intellectuals, workers, and peasants. When political freedoms were again curtailed at the outbreak of World War II, the Communist Party, now a well-disciplined organization, was forced back into hiding.

WORLD WAR II AND INDEPENDENCE

For five years during World War II, Indochina was a French-administered possession of Japan. On Sept.

22, 1940, Jean Decoux, the French governor-general appointed by the Vichy government after the fall of France to the Nazis, concluded an agreement with the Japanese that permitted the stationing of 30,000 Japanese troops in Indochina and the use of all major Vietnamese airports by the Japanese military. The agreement made Indochina the most important staging area for all Japanese military operations in Southeast Asia. The French administration cooperated with the Japanese occupation forces and was ousted only toward the end of the war (in March 1945), when the Japanese began to fear that the French forces might turn against them as defeat approached. After the French had been disarmed, Bao Dai, the last French-appointed emperor of Vietnam, was allowed to proclaim the independence of his country and to appoint a Vietnamese national government at Hue; however, all real power remained in the hands of the Japanese military commanders.

Meanwhile, in May 1941, at Ho Chi Minh's urging, the Communist Party formed a broad nationalist alliance under its leadership called the League for the Independence of Vietnam, which subsequently became known as the Viet Minh. Ho, returning to China to seek assistance, was arrested and imprisoned there by the Nationalist government. After his release he returned to Vietnam and began to cooperate with Allied forces by providing information on Japanese troop movements in Indochina. At the same time, he sought recognition of the Viet Minh as the legitimate representative of Vietnamese nationalist aspirations. When the Japanese surrendered in August 1945, the communist-led Viet Minh ordered a general uprising, and, with no one organized to oppose them, they were able to seize power in Hanoi. Bao Dai, the Vietnamese emperor, abdicated a few days later and declared his fealty to the newly proclaimed Democratic Republic of Vietnam.

The Communist Party had clearly gained the upper hand in its struggle to outmaneuver its disorganized rivals, such as the noncommunist VNQDD. The French, however, were determined to restore their colonial presence in Indochina and, with the aid of British occupation forces, seized control of Cochinchina. Thus, at the beginning of 1946, there were two Vietnams: a communist north and a noncommunist south.

THE FIRST INDOCHINA WAR

Negotiations between the French and Ho Chi Minh led to an agreement in March 1946 that appeared to promise a peaceful solution. Under the agreement

France would recognize the Viet Minh government and give Vietnam the status of a free state within the French Union. French troops were to remain in Vietnam, but they would be withdrawn progressively over five years. For a period in early 1946 the French cooperated with Ho Chi Minh as he consolidated the Viet Minh's dominance over other nationalist groups, in particular those politicians who were backed by the Chinese Nationalist Party.

Despite tactical cooperation between the French and the Viet Minh, their policies were irreconcilable: the French aimed to reestablish colonial rule, while Hanoi wanted total independence. French intentions were revealed in the decision of Georges-Thierry d'Argenlieu, the high commissioner for Indochina, to proclaim Cochinchina an autonomous republic in June 1946. Further negotiations did not resolve the basic differences between the French and the Viet Minh. In late November 1946 French naval vessels bombarded Haiphong, causing several thousand civilian casualties; the subsequent Viet Minh attempt to overwhelm French troops in Hanoi in December is generally considered to be the beginning of the First Indochina War.

Initially confident of victory, the French long ignored the real political cause of the war—the desire of the Vietnamese people, including their anticommunist leaders, to achieve unity and independence for their country. French efforts to deal with those issues were devious and ineffective. The French reunited Cochinchina with the rest of Vietnam in 1949, proclaiming the Associated State of Vietnam, and appointed the former emperor Bao Dai as chief of state. Most nationalists, however, denounced these maneuvers, and leadership in the struggle for independence from the French remained with the Viet Minh.

Meanwhile, the Viet Minh waged an increasingly successful guerrilla war, aided after 1949 by the new communist government of China. The United States, fearful of the spread of communism in Asia, sent large amounts of aid to the French. The French, however, were shaken by the fall of their garrison at Dien Bien Phu in May 1954 and agreed to negotiate an end to the war at an international conference in Geneva.

THE TWO VIETNAMS (1954–65)

The agreements concluded in Geneva between April and July 1954 (collectively called the Geneva Accords) were signed by French and Viet Minh representatives and provided for a cease-fire and temporary division of the country into two military zones at latitude 17 °N (popularly called the 17th parallel). All Viet Minh forces were to withdraw north of that line, and all French and Associated State of Vietnam troops were to remain south of it; permission was granted for refugees to move from one zone to the other during a limited time period. An international commission was established, composed of Canadian, Polish, and Indian members under an Indian chairman, to supervise the execution of the agreement.

This agreement left the Democratic Republic of Vietnam (henceforth called North Vietnam) in control of only the northern half of the country. The last of the Geneva Accords—called the Final Declaration—provided for elections, supervised by the commission, to be held throughout Vietnam in July 1956 in order to unify the country. Viet Minh leaders appeared certain to win these elections, and the United States and the leaders in the south would not approve or sign the Final Declaration; elections were never held.

In the midst of a mass migration of nearly one million people from the north to the south, the two Vietnams began to reconstruct their war-ravaged land. With assistance from the Soviet Union and China, the Hanoi government in the north embarked on an ambitious program of socialist industrialization; they also began to collectivize agriculture in earnest in 1958. In the south a new government appointed by Bao Dai began to build a new country. Ngo Dinh Diem, a Roman Catholic, was named prime minister and succeeded with American support in stabilizing the anticommunist regime in Saigon. He eliminated pro-French elements in the military and abolished the local autonomy of several religious-political groups. Then, in a government-controlled referendum in October 1955, Diem removed Bao Dai as chief of state and made himself president of the Republic of Vietnam (South Vietnam).

Diem's early success in consolidating power did not result in concrete political and economic achievements. Plans for land reform were sabotaged by entrenched interests. With the financial backing of the United States, the regime's chief energies were directed toward building up the military and a variety of intelligence and security forces to counter the still-influential Viet Minh. Totalitarian methods were directed against all who were regarded as opponents, and the favouritism shown to Roman Catholics alienated the majority Buddhist population. Loyalty to the president and his family was made a paramount duty, and Diem's brother, Ngo Dinh Nhu, founded an elitist underground organization to spy on officials, army officers, and prominent local citizens. Diem also refused to participate in the all-Vietnamese elections described in the Final Declaration. With support from the north, communist-led forces—popularly called the Viet Cong—launched an insurgency movement to seize power and reunify the country. The insurrection appeared close to succeeding, when Diem's army overthrew him in November 1963. Diem and his brother Nhu were killed in the coup.

THE SECOND INDOCHINA WAR

The government that seized power after Diem's ouster, however, was no more effective than its predecessor. A period of political instability followed, until the military firmly seized control in June 1965 under Nguyen Cao Ky. Militant Buddhists who had helped overthrow Diem strongly opposed Ky's government, but he was able to break their resistance. Civil liberties were restricted, political opponents—denounced as neutralists or pro-communists—were imprisoned, and political parties were allowed to operate only if they did not openly criticize government policy. The character of the regime remained largely unchanged after the presidential elections in September 1967, which led to the election of Gen. Nguyen Van Thieu as president.

No less evident than the oppressive nature of the Saigon regime was its inability to cope with the Viet

Cong. The insurgent movement, aided by a steady infiltration of weapons and advisers from the north, steadily built its fighting strength from about 30,000 men in 1963 to about 150,000 in 1965 when, in the opinion of many American intelligence analysts, the survival of the Saigon regime was seriously threatened. In addition, the political opposition in the south to Saigon became much more organized. The National Front for the Liberation of the South, popularly called the National Liberation Front (NLF), had been organized in late 1960 and within four years had a huge following.

Until 1960 the United States had supported the Saigon regime and its army only with military equipment, financial aid, and, as permitted by the Geneva Accords, 700 advisers for training the army. The number of advisers had increased to 17,000 by the end of 1963, and they were joined by an increasing number of American helicopter pilots. All of this assistance, however, proved insufficient to halt the advance of the Viet Cong, and in February 1965 U.S. Pres. Lyndon B. Johnson ordered the bombing of North Vietnam, hoping to prevent further infiltration of arms and troops into the south. Four weeks after the bombing began, the United States started sending troops into the south. By July the number of U.S. troops had reached 75,000; it continued to climb until

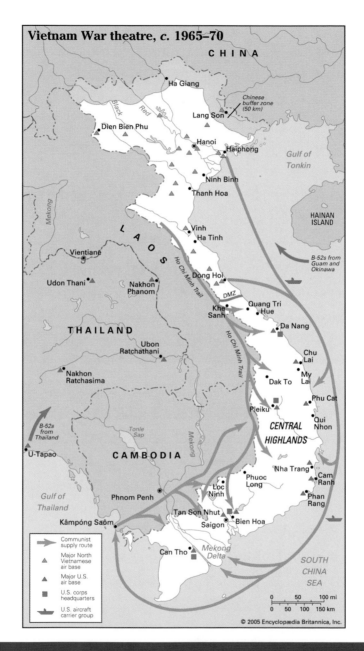

The United States first sent active combat units to Vietnam in 1965. All U.S. troops were withdrawn by 1973, though the war did not end until 1975.

it stood at more than 500,000 early in 1968. Fighting beside the Americans were some 600,000 regular South Vietnamese troops and regional and self-defense forces, as well as smaller contingents from South Korea, Thailand, Australia, and New Zealand.

Three years of intensive bombing of the north and fighting in the south, however, did not weaken the will and strength of the Viet Cong and their allies from the north. Infiltration of personnel and supplies down the famous Ho Chi Minh Trail continued at a high level, and regular troops from the north—now estimated at more than 100,000—played a growing role in the war. The continuing strength of the insurgent forces became evident in the so-called Tet Offensive that began in late January 1968, during which the Viet Cong and North Vietnamese attacked more than 100 cities and military bases, holding on to some for several weeks. After that, a growing conviction in the U.S. government that continuing the war at current levels was no longer politically acceptable led President Johnson to order a reduction of the bombing in the north. This decision opened the way for U.S. negotiations with Hanoi, which began in Paris in May 1968. After the bombing was halted over the entire north in November 1968, the Paris talks were enlarged to include representatives of the NLF and the Saigon regime.

The war continued under a new U.S. president, Richard M. Nixon, who began gradually to withdraw U.S. troops. Public opposition to the war, however, escalated after Nixon ordered attacks on the Ho Chi Minh Trail in Laos and on Viet Cong sanctuaries inside Cambodia. In the meantime, the peace talks went on in Paris.

Finally, in January 1973 a peace treaty was signed by the United States and all three Vietnamese parties (North Vietnam, South Vietnam, and the Viet Cong). It provided for the complete withdrawal of U.S. troops within 60 days and created a political process for the peaceful resolution of the conflict in the south. Nothing was said, however, about the presence of more than 100,000 North Vietnamese troops in South Vietnam.

The signing of the Paris Agreement did not bring an end to the fighting in Vietnam. The Saigon regime made a determined effort to eliminate the communist forces remaining in the south, while northern leaders continued to strengthen their military forces in preparation for a possible future confrontation. By late 1974 Hanoi had decided that victory could be achieved only through armed struggle, and early the next year North Vietnamese troops launched a major offensive against the south. Saigon's forces retreated in panic and disorder, and President Thieu

ordered the abandonment of several northern provinces. Thieu's effort to stabilize the situation was too
late, however, and on April 30, 1975, the communists
entered Saigon in triumph. The Second Indochina
War was finally at an end.

CHAPTER NINE

LAOS AND CAMBODIA

• •

T he neighboring modern countries of Laos and Cambodia were both under French rule until the mid-20th century. Interactions—sometimes hostile, sometimes hospitable—with the neighbouring Khmer (Cambodian), Siamese (Thai), and Myanmar (Burmese) kingdoms between the 5th and the mid-19th century indirectly imbued Laos with elements of Indian culture, including Buddhism, the religion now practiced by most of the population. Colonization by the French from the late 19th to the mid-20th century infused Laos with a European cultural element, which intensified throughout the country's embroilment in World War II and the Indochina wars, as well as a civil war of its own in the second half of the 20th century. Guided by Marxist-Leninist ideology, Laos emerged from the turmoil in 1975 as a communist country. The Khmer (Cambodian) empire reached its apex in the 12th century, a time marked by the construction of the massive temple complexes known as Angkor Wat and Bayon and the imperial capital of Angkor Thom. Following 400 years of decline, Cambodia became a French colony and during the 20th century experienced the turmoil of war, occupation by the Japanese, postwar independence, and political instability.

LAOS

During the 18th century the three Laotian states, which were continually at loggerheads, tried to maintain their independence from the Myanmar and Siamese kingdoms, both of which were contending for control of the western segment of continental Southeast Asia. Disunity weakened the Laotian kingdoms and inevitably caused them to fall prey to the Siamese.

UNDER FOREIGN RULE

Vien Chan, which had sided with Myanmar, was invaded (1778), annexed, and made a state subject to the Siamese (1782). Luang Prabang, which had supported Siam, was invaded by Myanmar (1752), which imposed its rule on it until being supplanted by the Siamese in 1778. In the south, Champassak, which had supported a Myanmar revolt against the Siamese, also was invaded (1778) and was transformed into a dependency of Siam. Each of these Lao kingdoms was placed under the control of a Siamese commissioner. The kings of Champassak, Vien Chan, and Luang Prabang were allowed to rule in their respective kingdoms but had to pay tribute to Bangkok. Their appointments to the throne were made in Bangkok.

The last king of Vien Chan, Chao Anou (also called Anouvong; ruled 1805–28), attempted to shake off this yoke. First, he strengthened the bonds of allegiance between Vien Chan and Vietnam (1806), whose influence in the region had grown to rival that of Siam. Next, he persuaded Bangkok to give his son the governorship of Champassak, thus extending his frontiers as far as the old southern boundaries of Lan Xang. Thinking that the British, who had just defeated Myanmar, were going to attack Siam, he led three armies against Bangkok (1827). The Siamese, however, regrouped their forces, marched on Vien Chan, and defeated Anou, who fled to Vietnam. Vien Chan was pillaged and destroyed. In 1828 Anou attempted another attack but was again defeated. Vien Chan was made a Siamese province.

For the Siamese the annexation of Vien Chan was the first step toward the creation of a great empire. They next extended their domain to the eastern bank of the Mekong to protect themselves from an eventual Vietnamese expansion westward, garrisoned Champassak (1846) and Luang Prabang (1885), and stationed troops as far as the Annamese Cordillera. Siamese expansion toward the northeast—where the mountain states were placed under the cosuzerainty of Vietnam and Luang Prabang—provoked the protests of the French, who had established a protectorate over Vietnam.

France entered into negotiations with Bangkok (1886) to define the Siamese-Vietnamese frontier and won the right to install a vice-consul in Luang Prabang. The office was entrusted to Auguste Pavie, who, partly because of his popularity with the Laotians, succeeded in winning Luang Prabang over to France. After a number of Franco-Siamese incidents in the Mekong River valley, French ships made a show of strength off Bangkok in 1893. Later that year, on the advice of the British, Siam withdrew from the eastern bank of the Mekong and gave official recognition to the French protectorate in the evacuated territory. French annexation was completed by treaties with Siam (called Thailand from 1939) in 1904 and 1907.

The French organized this territory as a protectorate (what came to be known as Indochine, or French Indochina), with its administrative centre at Vientiane, and allowed it autonomy in local matters. The kingdom of Luang Prabang survived, but the other provinces were placed under the direct authority of a French official. France paid little attention to Laos until the Japanese invaded mainland Southeast Asia during World War II; in 1941, under Japanese pressure, the Vichy government of German-occupied France restored to Thailand the territories France had acquired in 1904. In March 1945 the Japanese took outright administrative control of the remainder of French Indochina, and the following month the independence of Laos was proclaimed.

Two movements sprang up at that time. The first was anti-Japanese and was represented by the court of Luang Prabang and Prince Boun Oum of Champassak; the second was anti-French (the Free Laos movement, or Lao Issara), was located in Vientiane, and was led by Prince Phetsarath Ratanavongsa. These two movements remained in conflict until French troops returned, which in early 1946 compelled the supporters of the Lao Issara to flee to Thailand. France, in a temporary agreement, recognized the internal autonomy of Laos under the king of Luang Prabang, Sisavang Vong. Finally, after a constitution was promulgated and general elections were held, a Franco-Laotian convention was signed in July 1949 by which Laos was granted limited self-government within the French Union. All important power, however, remained in French hands.

Although many of the Lao Issara leaders were prepared to work with the French under this new arrangement, their decision was opposed by a more radical group led by Kaysone Phomvihan and Prince Souphanouvong. Under Souphanouvong's leadership a new political movement, the Pathet Lao ("Land of the Lao"), was proclaimed (1950); it joined forces with the Viet Minh of Vietnam in opposing the French. The Pathet Lao remained unreconciled when the French took further steps toward granting independence to Laos in October 1953 while still retaining control of all military matters in the kingdom. Between 1950 and early 1954 the Pathet Lao gained strength in northeastern Laos, and it had a firm grip on two of the country's provinces when the peace conference in Geneva brought the First Indochina War to an end.

LAOS AFTER THE GENEVA CONFERENCE, 1954–75

The Geneva Accords of 1954 marked the end of French rule in Southeast Asia. The participating countries (including France, Great Britain, the United States, China, and the Soviet Union) at the Geneva Conference agreed that all of Laos should come under the rule of the royal government and should not undergo partition (as did Vietnam). The agreements, however, did provide for two "regroupment zones" in provinces adjacent to what was then North Vietnam to allow the Pathet Lao forces to assemble. This resulted in the de facto control of those areas by the Laotian communists, while the rest of the country was ruled by the royal government.

The uneasy peace in Laos was short-lived, as hostilities broke out between leftist and rightist factions in 1959. Another conference in Geneva in May 1961 culminated in an agreement in July 1962 that called for the country to become neutral and for a tripartite government to be formed. The new government consisted of factions from the left (the Pathet Lao, who were linked to North Vietnam), the right (linked to Thailand and the United States), and neutrals (led by Prince Souvanna Phouma). Once again, however, the cease-fire was brief. The coalition had split apart by 1964, and the larger war centred in Vietnam subsequently engulfed Laos. In that expanded war Laos was viewed by the major protagonists as a sideshow.

An agreement negotiated in January 1973 by the United States and North Vietnam at Paris called

As premier of Laos, Souvanna Phouma was known for seeking to maintain Laotian neutrality in Southeast Asian affairs.

for a cease-fire in each of the countries of mainland Southeast Asia, but only in Laos was there peace. In February, just a month following the agreement, the Laotian factions signed the Vientiane Agreement, which provided again for a cease-fire and for yet another coalition government composed of factions from the left and right, presided over by Souvanna Phouma. As political control in Vietnam tipped toward the communists following the American departure from that country, the Pathet Lao gained political ascendancy in Laos. When the Vietnamese communists marched into Saigon (now Ho Chi Minh City, Viet.), and Phnom Penh, Camb., the right-wing forces in Laos lost heart, and most of their leaders fled, permitting a bloodless takeover by the Laotian communists in mid-1975. Though out of office, Souvanna Phouma remained an adviser to the new regime until his death in 1984. The Laotian communists proclaimed an end to the 600-year-old monarchy and established the Lao People's Democratic Republic (LPDR) in December 1975.

CAMBODIA

French control over Cambodia was an offshoot of French involvement in the neighbouring provinces of Vietnam. France's decision to advance into Cambodia

NORODOM

Norodom, also spelled Narottama (1834–1904), was the king of Cambodia from 1860 until 1904. Under duress, he placed his country under the control of the French in 1863.

Norodom was the eldest son of King Duong. He was educated in Bangkok, capital of the Thai kingdom, where he studied Pāli and Sanskrit Buddhist scriptures and the sacred canons of Theravāda Buddhism. The purpose of his early training was to strengthen ties between Siam (Thailand) and Cambodia.

Cambodia had been under the joint vassalage of Vietnam and Siam since 1802. According to established protocol, Cambodian kings were crowned jointly, with representatives of the two suzerains attending. When Duong died in 1860, Norodom was chosen the successor, but he remained uncrowned. The Thais, who held the symbols of Cambodian royalty—the crown, the sacred sword, and the royal seal—refused to release them, insisting that the newly elected king was their deputy and denying the Vietnamese the right to crown Norodom; thus the Siamese sought to undermine Vietnamese claims to Cambodia

(CONTINUED ON THE NEXT PAGE)

(CONTINUED FROM THE PREVIOUS PAGE)

and to assert their own private domination of the vassal state.

An attempted coup d'etat, led in 1861 by Norodom's half brother Si Votha, was put down with the aid of Thai troops. At this point the French, who had been ceded much of Cochinchina (southern Vietnam), sought to assert Vietnamese claims to Cambodian tribute, seeing the adjacent Cambodian provinces as future colonial possessions. The French forced Norodom to accept French protection early in 1863, but, before the agreement was ratified in Paris, Norodom signed a clandestine treaty with Siam on Aug. 11, 1863, which was ratified on Jan. 22, 1864. It made Norodom the viceroy of Siam and governor of Cambodia; Siam retained control of the Cambodian provinces of Bătdâmbâng and Siĕmréab. The French moved to stop Siam from asserting further claims over Cambodia and forced Siam to return the royal regalia, and Norodom was finally crowned at Oudong, Cambodia, in June 1864, with both French and Siamese officials attending. He was installed as king in Phnom Penh in 1866, and in 1867 Siam officially acknowledged the French protectorate over Cambodia. The French imposed land reforms, a reorganization of Cambodian military forces, and the abolition of slavery. Throughout Norodom's reign the French increased their domination of Cambodian affairs.

came only when it feared that British and Siamese expansion might threaten its access to the largely unmapped Mekong River, which, it assumed (incorrectly), would provide access to central China. In 1863 French naval officers from Vietnam persuaded King Norodom to sign a treaty that gave France control of Cambodia's foreign affairs. The effect of the treaty was to weaken Siamese protection. A French admiral participated in Norodom's coronation, with Siamese acquiescence, in 1864.

FRENCH PROTECTORATE

For the next 15 years or so, the French were not especially demanding, and Norodom benefited from French military help in putting down a series of rebellions. By the late 1870s, however, French officials in Cambodia were pressing for greater control over internal affairs. Shocked by what they regarded as the ineptitude and barbarity of Norodom's court and eager to turn a profit in Cambodia, they sought to introduce fiscal and judicial reforms. In doing that, the French knew that Norodom's half brother, Sisowath, who had ambitions for the throne, would cooperate with them. Norodom, however, resisted the reforms, which he correctly perceived as infringements on his power. Exasperated by his intransigence, the French in 1884 forced him at gunpoint to sign a document that virtually transformed Cambodia into a colony. Soon thereafter, provincial officials, feeling threatened, raised guerrilla armies to confront the French.

The rebellion, which lasted until mid-1886, was the only anti-French movement in the kingdom until after World War II. The French succeeded in suppressing it after agreeing to some concessions to the king, but Norodom's apparent victory was hollow. What the French had been unable to achieve by the

This 19th-century drawing depicts the invasion of Cambodia by French ships in 1861.

convention of 1884, they proceeded to gain through piecemeal action. As Norodom's health declined and as senior Cambodian officials came to see their interests increasingly linked with French power, the way was opened for greater French control. In 1897 the French representative in Phnom Penh assumed executive authority, reducing the king's power to a minimum. Norodom died, embittered and overtaken by events, in 1904.

The first 40 years of the French protectorate—whatever French motives may have been—had guaranteed the survival of the Cambodian state and had saved the kingdom from being divided between its two powerful neighbours. Norodom's successor, Sisowath (ruled 1904–27), was more cooperative with the French and presided benignly over the partial modernization of the kingdom. The northwestern provinces of Bătdâmbâng and Siĕmréab were returned to Cambodia by the Siamese in 1907. By the time Sisowath died, 20 years later, hundreds of miles of paved roads had been built, and thousands of acres of rubber plantations had been established by the French. Resistance to French rule, in sharp contrast to what was happening in neighbouring Vietnam, was almost nonexistent.

Sisowath's eldest son, Monivong, who reigned until 1941, was even more of a figurehead than his father had been. During the 1930s a railway opened between Phnom Penh and the Siamese (Thai) border, while the first Cambodian-language newspaper, *Nagara Vatta* ("Angkor Wat"), affiliated with the Buddhist Institute in Phnom Penh, conveyed a mildly nationalistic message to its readers.

WORLD WAR II AND ITS AFTERMATH

When Monivong died in 1941, Japanese forces had already occupied the component states of French Indochina, while leaving the French in administrative control. In those difficult circumstances, the French governor-general, Jean Decoux, placed Monivong's grandson, Prince Norodom Sihanouk, on the Cambodian throne. Decoux was guided by the expectation that Sihanouk, then only 18 years old, could be easily controlled. In the long run, the French underestimated Sihanouk's political skills, but for the remainder of World War II, he was a pliable instrument in their hands.

The effect of the Japanese occupation was less profound in Cambodia than it was elsewhere in Southeast Asia, but the overthrow of the French administration by the Japanese in March 1945, when the war was nearing its end, provided Cambodians with some opportunities for greater political autonomy. Pressed by the Japanese to do so, Sihanouk declared his country's independence, and for several months the government was led by Son Ngoc Thanh, a former editor of *Nagara Vatta*, who had been forced into exile in Japan in 1942.

In October 1945, after the war was over, the French returned to Indochina, arrested Son Ngoc Thanh, and reestablished their control. Cambodia soon became an "autonomous state within the French Union," with its own constitution and a handful of political parties, but real power remained in French hands. There were, however, several significant political developments between 1945 and the achievement of complete independence in 1953, the most important of which was the confrontation between Sihanouk and his advisers on the one hand and the leaders of the pro-independence Democratic Party, which dominated the National Assembly, on the other. Cambodia was poorly prepared for parliamentary democracy, and the French were unwilling to give the National Assembly genuine power. The Democrats, for their part, suffered from internal dissension. The death in 1947 of their leader, Prince Yuthevong, was a severe blow, exacerbated by the assassination of Yuthevong's heir apparent, Ieu

Koeuss, in early 1950. Outside the parliament, Son Ngoc Thanh, released from exile in France in 1951, formed a dissident movement, the Khmer Serei ("Free Khmer"), that opposed both Sihanouk and the French.

In June 1952 Sihanouk assumed control of the government. Many Cambodian students in France, among them Saloth Sar (who would become the future communist dictator Pol Pot), objected to Sihanouk's move, but inside Cambodia the king remained extremely popular. His self-styled "Royal Crusade," consisting of a tour of several countries to elicit their support, wrested political independence from the French, who by the end of 1953 were eager to compromise. Sihanouk's success discredited the communist-dominated guerrilla movement in Cambodia—associated with the Viet Minh of Vietnam—and Son Ngoc Thanh's anticommunist Khmer Serei.

INDEPENDENCE

Sihanouk's government was recognized as the sole legitimate authority within Cambodia at the Geneva Conference convened in 1954 to reach a political settlement to the First Indochina War (the Geneva Accords). That decision prevented the Viet Minh from gaining any regional power in Cambodia, as they did in Laos.

While Democrats and communists alike recognized Sihanouk's role in gaining Cambodia's independence, they opposed his increasing authoritarianism. Sihanouk abdicated the throne in March 1955 in favour of his father, Norodom Suramarit, and formed a mass political movement, the Sangkum Reastr Niyum ("People's Socialist Community"), whose members were forbidden to belong to other political parties. The effect of the move was to draw thousands of people away from the Democrats, who had expected to win the national elections scheduled for later in the year. When the elections took place, amid widely reported abuses by Sihanouk's police, the Sangkum won every seat in the National Assembly.

Sihanouk became the central figure in Cambodian politics from then until his overthrow in 1970, as prime minister and—after his father's death in 1960, when no new monarch was named—as head of state. Overt political life was strictly controlled by the prince, his colleagues, and the police; Cambodian communists, a marginal group of fewer than a thousand members, operated clandestinely and enjoyed little success. In 1963 Saloth Sar, a schoolteacher who was also secretary of the Communist Party, fled Phnom Penh and took refuge in the forests along the Vietnamese border; from there he built the organization that later would be known as the Khmer Rouge.

Sihanouk was widely revered in Cambodia until the late 1960s, when opposition to his rule

Prince Norodom Sihanouk of Cambodia (*right*) meets with U.S. Pres. John F. Kennedy in New York City, 1961.

intensified. He saw Thailand and what was then South Vietnam as the greatest threats to Cambodia's survival. Those two countries were allied with the United States, which the prince disliked. At the same time, Sihanouk feared the eventual success of the Vietnamese communists in their war against South Vietnam and the United States, and he dreaded the prospect of a unified Vietnam under communist control. To gain some freedom to maneuver, he proclaimed a policy of neutrality in international affairs. Sihanouk broke off relations with the United States in 1965, convinced of American involvement in two South Vietnamese-backed plots against the Cambodian state in 1959 and encouraged in his anti-Americanism by the French president, Charles de Gaulle, whom he idolized. Soon afterward he concluded secret agreements with the Vietnamese communists, who were allowed to station troops on Cambodian territory in outlying districts as long as they did not interfere with Cambodian civilians. The secret agreement protected Sihanouk's army from attacks by the Vietnamese but compromised his neutralist policies. After 1965, when the war in Vietnam intensified, he also edged toward an alliance with China.

Cambodia's internal politics after 1965 developed in a complex fashion. Elections in 1966, the first since 1951 not to be stage-managed by the prince, brought in a majority of National Assembly members who owed little or nothing to Sihanouk himself. Although the prince was still a revered figure among the rural populace, he became increasingly unpopular with the educated elite. Conservatives resented his break with the United States and his seemingly pro-communist foreign policy, while Cambodian radicals opposed his internal policies, which were economically conservative and intolerant of dissent. A rebellion in Bătdâmbâng province in 1967, manipulated by local communists, convinced the prince that the greatest threat to his regime came from the radical sector, and without hesitation he began using severe measures—including imprisonment without trial, assassinations, and the burning of villages—to impose his will.

By 1969 Sihanouk's grip on Cambodian politics had loosened, and conflict between his army and communist guerrillas, especially in the northeast, had increased. Some anticommunist ministers led by Prince Sirik Matak and General Lon Nol plotted to depose Sihanouk, whose credibility with radicals had evaporated following his renewal of diplomatic relations with the United States.

Sihanouk's elaborate policy of juggling major powers against each other had failed. Matak and Lon Nol worked closely with anticommunists in South Vietnam, including Son Ngoc Thanh, whose Khmer Serei movement had gained recruits among the Khmer-speaking minority in Vietnam.

CONCLUSION

Despite the fact that western colonialism did not come to much of East and Southeast Asia until the 19th century, it had a significant impact on the region. Thailand was the only country not to be formally colonized. China, though it likewise was not brought under foreign rule, was forced to sign many unequal treaties with western countries, which opened the region to more western influence. Also at the end of the 19th century, Japan became an imperial power, creating an empire that at its peak included Korea, inner Mongolia, coastal China, mainland Southeast Asia, the Philippines, and Borneo. After Japan's defeat in World War II, the Allied powers were also weakened and began to lose control of their colonies in Southeast Asia: Indonesia gained independence from the Netherlands; the Philippines from the United States; Indochina from France; and Burma and Malaya from Britain. However, the scars of colonialism lingered across the region for many decades. The last vestiges of western colonialism in East and Southeast Asia were finally erased in 1997, when Hong Kong and Macau returned to Chinese rule.

barangay A unit of administration in Philippine society consisting of from 50 to 100 families under a headman.

cease-fire A suspension of active hostilities.

Culture System A revenue system in the Dutch East Indies (Indonesia) that forced farmers to pay revenue to the treasury of the Netherlands in the form of export crops or compulsory labour.

datu A local headman in many parts of central Malaysia and the southern Philippines.

entrepôt A place serving as an intermediary center for the collection and distribution of goods.

Ethical Policy A program introduced by the Dutch in the East Indies at the turn of the 20th century aimed at promoting the welfare of the indigenous Indonesians (Javanese).

governor-general A governor of high rank, especially one who governs a large territory (such as a country) or has lieutenant or deputy governors under him or her.

guerrilla One who carries on or assists in an irregular war or engages in irregular warfare in connection with a regular war, especially a member of an independent band engaged in predatory excursions in wartime.

insular Of or relating to an island.

Javzandamba A religious leader in Mongolia.

nationalism Loyalty and devotion to a nation; especially an attitude, feeling, or belief characterized by a sense of national consciousness, an exaltation of one nation above all others, and an emphasis on loyalty to and the promotion of the culture and interests (as political independence) of one nation as opposed to subordinate areas or other nations and supranational groups.

opium A drug that consists of the dried milky juice of the opium poppy obtained from incisions made in the unripe capsules of the plant. It is a stimulant narcotic poison that usually produces a feeling of well-being, hallucinations, and drowsiness.

protectorate The relationship of superior authority assumed by one power or state over a dependent political unit.

sphere of influence A territorial area within which the political influence or the interests of one nation are held to be more or less paramount; a region more or less under the control of a nation but not constituting a formally recognized protectorate.

sultanate The office, dignity, or power of a sultan, a king, or ruling sovereign.

tariff A schedule, system, or scheme of duties imposed by a government on imported or exported goods for the production of revenue, for the artificial fostering of home industries, or as a means of coercing foreign governments to grant reciprocity privileges.

BIBLIOGRAPHY

JAPAN

Useful works on the opening of Japan and the fall of the shogunate include Matthew C. Perry, *Narrative of the Expedition of an American Squadron to the China Seas and Japan*, 3 vol. (1856, reissued 1967); Oliver Statler, *Shimoda Story* (1969, reprinted 1986); Grace Fox, *Britain and Japan, 1858–1883* (1969); and W.G. Beasley (trans. and ed.), *Select Documents on Japanese Foreign Policy, 1853–1868* (1955, reissued 1967).

Works dealing with imperial Japan include Akira Iriye, *After Imperialism: The Search for a New Order in the Far East, 1921–1931* (1965, reissued 1990); Ramon H. Myers and Mark R. Peattie (eds.), *The Japanese Colonial Empire, 1895–1945* (1984); James B. Crowley, *Japan's Quest for Autonomy: National Security and Foreign Policy, 1930–1938* (1966); and Francis Clifford Jones, *Japan's New Order in East Asia: Its Rise and Fall, 1937–45* (1954, reprinted 1978).

Studies of the wartime period include Sadako N. Ogata, *Defiance in Manchuria: The Making of Japanese Foreign Policy, 1931–1932* (1964, reprinted 1984); a four-volume series, *Japan's Road to the Pacific War*, ed. by James William Morley, *Deter-*

rent Diplomacy: Japan, Germany, and the USSR, 1935–1940 (1976), *The Fateful Choice: Japan's Advance into Southeast Asia, 1939–1941* (1980), *Japan Erupts: The London Naval Conference and the Manchurian Incident, 1928–1932* (1984), and *The China Quagmire: Japan's Expansion on the Asian Continent, 1933–1941* (1983), all trans. from Japanese; Dorothy Borg and Shumpei Okamoto (eds.), *Pearl Harbor as History: Japanese-American Relations, 1931–1941* (1973); Ronald H. Spector, *Eagle Against the Sun: The American War with Japan* (1985); Robert J.C. Butow, *Japan's Decision to Surrender* (1954, reissued 1967); Thomas R.H. Havens, *Valley of Darkness: The Japanese People and World War Two* (1978, reprinted 1986); and John W. Dower, *War Without Mercy: Race and Power in the Pacific War* (1986, reissued 1993).

Important postwar studies include Masataka Kosaka, *100 Million Japanese: The Postwar Experience* (1972, reissued as *A History of Postwar Japan*, 1982); Andrew Gordon (ed.), *Postwar Japan as History* (1993); Robert E. Ward and Sakamoto Yoshikazu (Yoshikazu Sakamoto) (eds.), *Democratizing Japan: The Allied Occupation* (1987); and Kazuo Kawai, *Japan's American Interlude* (1960, reprinted 1979).

CHINA

External challenges to the Qing are surveyed in Masataka Banno, *China and the West, 1858–1861: The Origins of the Tsungli Yamen* (1964); Hsin-pao Chang, *Commissioner Lin and the Opium War* (1964, reissued 1970); John K. Fairbank, *Trade and Diplomacy on the China Coast,* 2 vol. (1953, reissued in 1 vol., 1969); Immanuel C.Y. Hsu, *China's Entrance into the Family of Nations: The Diplomatic Phase, 1858–1880* (1960); Peter Ward Fay, *The Opium War, 1840–1842* (1976, reprinted 1997); and Frederic Wakeman, Jr., *Strangers at the Gate: Social Disorder in South China, 1839–1861* (1966, reprinted 1997).

Studies of the Taiping Rebellion include Vincent Y.C. Shih, *The Taiping Ideology: Its Sources, Interpretations, and Influences* (1967, reprinted 1972); Franz H. Michael and Chang Chung-li, *The Taiping Rebellion: History and Documents*, 3 vol. (1966–71); and Albert Feuerwerker, *Rebellion in Nineteenth-Century China* (1975); and among those for the Nian Rebellion are Siang-tseh Chiang, *The Nien Rebellion* (1954, reprinted 1967); S.Y. Teng, *The Nien Army and Their Guerrilla Warfare, 1851–1868* (1961, reprinted 1984); and Elizabeth J. Perry, *Rebels and Revolutionaries in North China, 1845–1945* (1980).

Studies of the Boxer Rebellion include Paul A. Cohen, *China and Christianity: The Missionary Movement and the Growth of Chinese Antiforeignism, 1860–1870* (1963), and *History in Three Keys: The Boxers as Event, Experience, and Myth* (1997); Victor Purcell, *The Boxer Uprising* (1963, reprinted 1974); and Joseph W. Esherick, *The Origins of the Boxer Uprising* (1987).

Jung-Fang Tsai, *Hong Kong in Chinese History: Community and Social Unrest in the British Colony, 1842–1913* (1993); and Elizabeth Sinn, *Power and Charity: A Chinese Merchant Elite in Colonial Hong Kong* (2003), focus on the Chinese elite and working classes during the colonial period in Hong Kong. Norman Miners, *Hong Kong Under Imperial Rule, 1912–1941* (1987), addresses the political and economic issues of the period before the Japanese occupation.

KOREA

Studies of the colonial period in Korea include Martina Deuchler, *Confucian Gentlemen and Barbarian Envoys: The Opening of Korea, 1875–1885* (1977); George Alexander Lensen, *Balance of Intrigue: International Rivalry in Korea & Manchuria, 1884–1899*, 2 vol. (1982); Vipan Chandra, *Imperialism, Resistance, and Reform in Late Nineteenth-Century*

Korea: Enlightenment and the Independence Club (1988); Homer B. Hulbert, *The Passing of Korea* (1906, reprinted with a new foreword, 1969), showing how Korea was deprived of its sovereignty toward the end of the 19th century amid the conflict of the great powers in Korea; Chong-sik Lee, *The Politics of Korean Nationalism* (1963), a comprehensive study of the nationalist movement during Japanese colonial rule; Andrew J. Grajdanzev (A.J. Grad), *Modern Korea* (1944, reprinted 1978), a critique of Japanese imperial rule in Korea; Carter J. Eckert, *Offspring of Empire: The Koch'ang Kims and the Colonial Origins of Korean Capitalism, 1876–1945* (1991), a well-written study arguing that Korean capitalism first arose during the colonial period; and Michael Edson Robinson, *Cultural Nationalism in Colonial Korea, 1920–1925* (1988).

MONGOLIA

The period of Manchu domination of Mongolia is well covered in Charles R. Bawden, *The Modern History of Mongolia*, 2nd rev. ed., with an afterword by Alan J.K. Sanders (1989; reissued 2002); and in M. Sanjdorj, *Manchu Chinese Colonial Rule in Northern Mongolia*, trans. from Mongolian and annotated by Urgunge Onon (1980).

INDONESIA

M.C. Ricklefs, *Jogjakarta Under Sultan Mangkubumi, 1749–1792: A History of the Division of Java* (1974), examines 18th-century Javanese politics against the background of the Dutch presence. Jean Gelman Taylor, *The Social World of Batavia: European and Eurasian in Dutch Asia* (1983), explores European adaptation to the local scene in the 18th and 19th centuries. Clive Day, *The Policy and Administration of the Dutch in Java* (1904, reprinted as *The Dutch in Java*, 1972), remains an interesting treatment of the Cultivation System and Liberal Policy. The best survey in English of Dutch economic policies in the 19th and 20th centuries is still J.S. Furnivall, *Netherlands India* (1939, reissued 1983).

The Japanese occupation is examined in Harry J. Benda, *The Crescent and the Rising Sun: Indonesian Islam Under the Japanese Occupation, 1942–1945* (1958, reissued 1983); and Benedict R. O'G. Anderson, *Some Aspects of Indonesian Politics Under the Japanese Occupation: 1944–1945* (1961). Anderson's *Java in a Time of Revolution: Occupation and Resistance, 1944–1946* (1972, reissued 2006), gives a close study of the opening period of revolution.

George McTurnan Kahin, *Nationalism and Revolution in Indonesia* (1952, reissued 2003), remains the standard study of the rise of nationalism and the struggle for independence. Anthony Reid, *The Indonesian National Revolution, 1945–1950* (1974, reprinted 1986), is a more recent survey of the revolution. Ruth T. McVey, *The Rise of Indonesian Communism* (1965, reissued 2006), is an authoritative history of the Indonesian Communist Party to the revolts of 1926–27. Bernhard Dahm, *Sukarno and the Struggle for Indonesian Independence* (1969; originally published in German, 1966), explores the development of Sukarno's thinking up to 1945. Taufik Abdullah (ed.), *The Heartbeat of Indonesian Revolution* (1997), analyzes the Indonesian national revolution from a comparative perspective.

The standard account of the early years of independence is Herbert Feith, *The Decline of Constitutional Democracy in Indonesia* (1962, reissued 2007). Daniel S. Lev, *The Transition to Guided Democracy* (1966), carries the story from 1957 to 1959; and Rex Mortimer, *Indonesian Communism Under Sukarno* (1974, reissued 2006), continues it from 1959 to 1965. J.D. Legge, *Sukarno: A Political Biography*, new ed. (2004), also covers the period.

PHILIPPINES

Studies of important themes and historical periods are John Leddy Phelan, *The Hispanization of the Philippines: Spanish Aims and Filipino Responses, 1565–1700* (1959, reissued 1967), on the early Spanish era; Vicente L. Rafael, *Contracting Colonialism: Translation and Christian Conversion in Tagalog Society Under Early Spanish Rule* (1988, reissued 1993); Alfred W. McCoy and Ed. C. de Jesus (eds.), *Philippine Social History: Global Trade and Local Transformations* (1982), on the economic and social developments of the 19th and 20th centuries; John N. Schumacher, *The Propaganda Movement, 1880–1895: The Creation of a Filipino Consciousness, the Makers of Revolution*, rev. ed. (1997); Reynaldo Clemeña Ileto, *Pasyon and Revolution: Popular Movements in the Philippines, 1840–1910* (1979, reprinted 1997), on the cultural roots of the Philippine Revolution; and Norman G. Owen, *Prosperity Without Progress: Manila Hemp and Material Life in the Colonial Philippines* (1984).

The American conquest and subsequent colonial rule is covered in Brian McAllister Linn, *The Philippine War, 1899–1902* (2000); Glenn Anthony May, *Battle for Batangas: A Philippine Province at*

War (1991); Resil B. Mojares, *The War Against the Americans: Resistance and Collaboration in Cebu, 1899–1906* (1999); Peter W. Stanley, *A Nation in the Making: The Philippines and the United States, 1899–1921* (1974); Michael Cullinane, *Ilustrado Politics: Filipino Elite Responses to American Rule, 1898–1908* (2003); and Frank Hindman Golay, *Face of Empire: United States–Philippine Relations, 1898–1946* (1997).

Ricardo Trota José (ed.), *World War II and the Japanese Occupation* (2006); and David Joel Steinberg, *Philippine Collaboration in World War II* (1967), provide useful overviews of the Japanese occupation during the Pacific war. Critical studies of postwar political, economic, and social conditions include David Wurfel, *Filipino Politics: Development and Decay* (1988); Amando Doronila, *The State, Economic Transformation, and Political Change in the Philippines, 1946–1972* (1992); and Eva-Lotta E. Hedman and John T. Sidel, *Philippine Politics and Society in the Twentieth Century: Colonial Legacies, Post-Colonial Trajectories* (2000).

MALAYSIA AND MYANMAR

Steven Runciman, *The White Rajahs: A History of Sarawak from 1841 to 1946* (1960, reissued 1992);

and Robert Pringle, *Rajahs and Rebels: The Ibans of Sarawak Under Brooke Rule, 1841–1941* (1970), provide excellent coverage of the Brooke era. William R. Roff, *The Origins of Malay Nationalism*, 2nd ed. (1994), is a stimulating work that explores Malay society in the colonial years. Victor Purcell, *The Chinese in Malaya* (1948, reissued 1967), though somewhat dated, remains an important general survey. R.S. Milne and Diane K. Mauzy, *Politics and Government in Malaysia*, rev. ed. (1980), offers a particularly thorough account of the late colonial and early independence periods. A good survey of the country's growth in the few decades following independence is John Gullick, *Malaysia: Economic Expansion and National Unity* (1981).

Analyses of colonial conflicts in Burma include Oliver B. Pollak, *Empires in Collision: Anglo-Burmese Relations in the Mid-Nineteenth Century* (1979), which treats British policy and its effects on later colonization; and Dorothy Woodman, *The Making of Burma* (1962), which reveals theretofore secret British decisions in the colonization of Burma.

VIETNAM

Milton E. Osborne, *The French Presence in Cochinchina and Cambodia: Rule and Response (1859–*

1905) (1969), analyzes French policies during the first stages of colonial rule. Hue-Tam Ho Tai, *Radicalism and the Origins of the Vietnamese Revolution* (1992, reissued 1996), plumbs the sources of anticolonial thought. David G. Marr, *Vietnamese Anticolonialism, 1885–1925* (1971), is a sensitive account, *Vietnamese Tradition on Trial, 1920–1945* (1981, reissued 1984), explores the social and intellectual changes taking place under colonial rule, and *Vietnam 1945: The Quest for Power* (1995, reprinted 1997), explains the August Revolution. Ellen J. Hammer, *The Struggle for Indochina* (1954, reissued 1969), dramatically treats the final stages of French rule.

Huynh Kim Khánh, *Vietnamese Communism, 1925–1945* (1982, reissued 1986), is the definitive account of the rise of the Vietnamese communist movement. Alexander B. Woodside, *Community and Revolution in Modern Vietnam* (1976), argues that the search for community is a key factor in the Vietnamese revolution. Thomas Hodgkin, *Vietnam* (1981), recounts in detail the background of the Vietnamese revolutionary struggle. Bernard B. Fall, *The Two Viet-Nams*, 2nd rev. ed. (1967, reprinted 1984), dated but still useful, examines the period after the division of the country. William J. Duiker, *Sacred War: Nationalism and Revolution in a Divided Vietnam* (1995), focuses on Vietnamese communist perspectives and strategy, and his *Ho Chi Minh* (2000) is the most comprehensive account of the communist leader's life. David W.P. Elliott, *The Vietnamese War: Revolution and Social Change in the Mekong Delta* (2003), is a detailed analysis of communist techniques and popular responses; while Truong Nhu Tang, David Chanoff, and Doan Van Toai, *A Vietcong Memoir* (1985; also published as *Journal of a Vietcong*, 1986), is a firsthand account of the organization. Ken Post, *Revolution, Socialism, and Nationalism in Vietnam*, 5 vol. (1989–94), is a Marxist interpretation of the Vietnamese revolution.

LAOS AND CAMBODIA

Arthur J. Dommen, *Laos: Keystone of Indochina* (1985), is a brief general history, and his *Conflict in Laos*, rev. ed. (1971), a political history, focuses primarily on the period from the early 1950s to 1970. Also useful is Martin Stuart-Fox, *Historical Dictionary of Laos*, 2nd ed. (2001). Joseph J. Zasloff (ed.), *Laos: Beyond the Revolution* (1991), discusses the early years of the LPDR. MacAlister Brown and Joseph J. Zasloff, *Apprentice Revolutionaries: The Communist Movement in Laos, 1930–1985* (1986), provides a political analysis of the rise of communism.

Three general introductions to Cambodia are Russell R. Ross (ed.), *Cambodia: A Country Study*, 3rd ed. (1990); David P. Chandler, *The Land and People of Cambodia* (1991); and Ian Mabbett and David P. Chandler, *The Khmers* (1995). Helen Jarvis (compiler), *Cambodia* (1997), an annotated bibliography, is an excellent guide to sources on Cambodia. Justin Corfield and Laura Summers, *Historical Dictionary of Cambodia* (2003), is also a valuable reference work. David P. Chandler, *A History of Cambodia*, 3rd ed. (2000), traces the country's history from its beginnings up to the 21st century and is supplemented by his *The Tragedy of Cambodian History* (1991), an account of events since World War II.